Alistair McDowal
Pomona

'It's *all* real. All of it. Everything bad is real.'

–Moe

Alistair McDowall's *Pomona* was first staged in 2014 and won properly startling, and startled, acclaim. Its edgeland setting permits a surrealistic disengagement of linear forms of time, which is both dreamlike and wildly funny; nightmarish and ominously enveloping. The play has as its imaginative springboard a landscape which is both real and surreal. It offers an unforgettable journey into radical uncertainty, alongside unpredictable action that presents and questions the forms by which all too much of British life is lived.

Rabey offers us a wild plunge into a modern English urban rabbit hole, a haunting and bewildering high-stakes hunt for meaning and value, set in a gothic noir Manchester, possibly dystopian (or possibly not).

David Ian Rabey is Professor of Drama and Theatre Studies in the Department of Theatre, Film and Television Studies at Aberystwyth University, UK.

The Fourth Wall

The Fourth Wall series is a growing collection of short books on famous plays. Its compact format perfectly suits the kind of fresh, engaging criticism that brings a play to life.

Each book in this series selects one play or musical as its subject and approaches it from an original angle, seeking to shed light on an old favourite or break new ground on a modern classic. These lively, digestible books are a must for anyone looking for new ideas on the major works of modern theatre.

www.routledge.com/performance/series/4THW

Also available in this series

Coming soon

Alistair McDowall's
Pomona

David Ian Rabey

Routledge
Taylor & Francis Group

LONDON AND NEW YORK

First published 2018
by Routledge
2 Park Square, Milton Park, Abingdon, Oxon OX14 4RN

and by Routledge
711 Third Avenue, New York, NY 10017

Routledge is an imprint of the Taylor & Francis Group, an informa business

British Library Cataloguing-in-Publication Data
A catalogue record for this book is available from the British Library

Library of Congress Cataloging-in-Publication Data
A catalog record for this title has been requested

ISBN: 978-1-138-23529-8 (pbk)
ISBN: 978-1-315-30495-3 (ebk)

Typeset in Bembo
by Apex CoVantage, LLC

Contents

Acknowledgements

This one is dedicated to Dr Lara Maleen Kipp, to memories of David Blumfield and to the active ingredients in my 2016 Aberystwyth University production of *Pomona*: Rose Robinson (Ollie), Gwynedd Price and Fern Ward (Fay), Holly Moseley and Emily Power (Fay), Alex Cartwright and Bryony Morrison (Keaton), Fraser Brown and Patrick Young (Zeppo), Savannah Robinson and Josh Miles (Charlie), Harriet Carter and Callum Green (Moe), Chloe Matthews and Kaitlan Saffin (assistant directors), Matthew Cornerford Dunbar (stage manager), Paige Brookes (lighting design), Agata Sikorska (sound design), Ashleigh Parish Moir (costume and make-up design), under the supervision of Rebecca Mitchell (technical manager), Simon Banham (scenography tutor).

Further thanks to Dan Rebellato, whose *Spilled Ink* blog posting first alerted me to *Pomona*; Charmian Savill for prompting some formulations in the last chapter, and much more; Alistair McDowall, for approval of quotations and brief observations of detail on draft material; Ben Piggott for his constructive observations and acceptance of this project, the first book-length analysis of McDowall's theatre, which should not be the last. . . .

Roll the dice.

Note: all in-text references to *Pomona* refer to the Bloomsbury edition (London and New York, 2015).

Introduction

Darkness on the edge of town

To shake off the maddening and wearying limitations of time and space and natural law – to be linked with the vast *outside* – to come close to the knighted and abysmal secrets of the infinite and the ultimate – surely such a thing was worth the risk of one's life, soul and sanity!

–H. P. Lovecraft, 'The Whisperer in Darkness'
(Lovecraft, 1999: 237)

'Tonight feels like a board game co-designed by M. C. Escher on a bender and Stephen King in a fever' writes David Mitchell in *Slade House* (Mitchell, 2015: 119). His protagonist might be describing or entering *Pomona*: Alistair McDowall's play, inspired by a region of Manchester which has a dedicated tram stop only 15 minutes' ride from Manchester's central Piccadilly rail station. The Pomona region is best visited by day, as after dark there are no streetlights in its wilder ranges: it is a place where, if investigated, you literally outwalk the furthest city light.

Walk left, disembarking from the metro station, and you will see how tidy new gated factories try to outstare the

opposite side of the canal towpath, which harbours the bot-
tles and mattresses of rough sleepers in its foliage. Walk right,
and you enter a landscape which could serve as a site-specific
walking dramatization of Cormac McCarthy's apocalyptic
novel *The Road* (2006). Extravagantly strange vegetation
pushes up through split concrete to reclaim a post-industrial
landscape of buckled gates, tangled wire and mysterious pot-
holes leading down into – what? Sewers? Or. . . ?

Under a viaduct, a nocturnal encampment for rough sleepers is manifested by a cluster of furniture (including a bizarre
chair, awaiting the customer of a demonic barber or dentist).
This is the region described in the first scene of the play: 'It's
a hole./A hole in the middle of the city./Looks like what
the world'll be in a few thousand years' (19). See Image 1.1.

So what happens in Alistair McDowall's play, which bears
this place's name and draws the audience steadily into a
nightmare vision of its landscape? Dan Rebellato makes an
honourable attempt at summary:

> So, describe *Pomona* then. Well that's already tough. I'd
> say that a woman goes missing in Manchester and her
> identical twin tries to enlist help to find her. I think the
> missing woman has problems with drugs and debts and
> becomes a prostitute and then falls in with a gang who get
> her to film violent porn movies. I think she then disap-
> pears one day and her friend in the brothel discovers that
> their boss has their blood-type information on her com-
> puter. I think their boss then enlists two security guards
> to kill the friend, perhaps acting on the authority of The
> Girl, a mythical unnamed figure who controls everything
> and I mean everything. I think the guards kidnap the
> friend but bungle it and are forced to fake a violent attack.

Image 1.1 That is the real Pomona: an unusually surreal place

Photo of Pomona, 31 October 2015, by Charmian Savill, used by permission

I think that inadvertently one of the guards dies from the wounds administered in the fake attack. I think the sister looking for her twin eventually stumbles upon an underground hospital where the disappeared are being kept, their organs harvested, their bodies used as baby farms. I think the twin escapes but her sister does not. However, some or all of this might just be events taking place in a RPG, dungeon-mastered by Charlie. It could be a dream or a nightmare or a fiction or it might all be real. I'll be honest, I spent some of the performance confused, much of it uneasy, moments of it actually frightened, but at no point did I doubt that what I was watching was somehow necessary, urgent, inevitable, and about us now. Moe, one of the guards, announces 'It's *all* real./All of it./Everything bad is real.'

(*Pomona*, p. 101; Rebellato, 2014)

Where did this *thing* spring from? Alistair McDowall says:

I never have an answer as to where a play has come from, but I can show you some of the elements: some of the mess that was orbiting at the time.

Usually a character or maybe a scene or just an image occurs to me – in *Pomona* it was this guy in a car with the chicken nuggets circling the M60 – and I'll carry it round in my head with me for a long time, at the same time accruing notes and scraps of dialogue that spring from it and other places, until eventually maybe I realise: this is a ghost story, or maybe it's not, this is a detective story, or maybe it's both? And then maybe I'll read some Raymond Chandler or watch *Chinatown* (I always thought *Pomona* was like a horror version of *Chinatown*), try and find pieces of the tonal world I want the play to live in. And music is very important at this stage, most of the plays have a song, or a couple of songs that I'll listen to repeatedly, finding the way the play feels, the beat of it . . . I quite often draw little cartoons of the characters, or some of the images in the play. Eventually I've gathered heaps of this stuff, and then I'll start putting it into 'pots', arranging it so structures start to appear, and I'll write out the structure again and again and again.

I try to get to a point where I've worked so long doing everything else that I become desperate to write, I can't do anything else. Then (hopefully), the play can pour out of its own volition.

(McDowall, 2016)

On the surface, *Pomona* starts out evoking the appeal, form and tropes of the detective story, in which we observe a protagonist, on an investigative quest for knowledge, and we share her or his perspective (either completely or predominantly) as complex tangles of corruption are uncovered. However, *Pomona* has dimensions which may exceed even those detected in its forerunner, Roman Polanski's 1974 film *Chinatown*: dimensions which Michael Eaton significantly identifies as simultaneously political (about the nature of power), sexual (about the nature of gender), metaphysical (about the nature of evil), psychological (about the nature of the self) and philosophical (about the nature of knowledge) (Eaton, 1997: 43).

Pomona evokes the shockingly violent world of the crime thriller and the (apparently) nihilistic *film noir*, shot through with savage black humour. But it does so with a political purpose: in order to develop a scenario of the fiscal logic of human objectification, carried through to an underground trade in baby farming and organ harvesting. This scenario may also bring to mind Kazuo Ishiguro's dystopian novel *Never Let Me Go* (2005), but even more troublingly locates in Manchester events which are more regularly and horrifyingly documented in other countries (just as Sarah Kane's 1995 *Blasted* relocated atrocities from Bosnia to tear through the would-be soporific placelessness of a hotel room in Leeds, collapsing dramatic *space* in dramatic *time*). Indeed, since *Pomona* was performed in Manchester, the existence of subterranean communities in the bowels of the city has been nationally reported by journalist Dean Kirby in *The Independent* newspaper (Kirby, 2016). Some of Manchester's shockingly large number of destitute and homeless "rough sleepers" have been discovered living in the relative shelter, but in appalling pitch-black conditions, afforded by an underground cave, near the River Irwell. So aspects of what might be initially dismissed as science fiction and apocalyptic dystopia are already apparent in present-day social upheavals and their consequences. Theatre is a particularly good imaginative form for exploring consequences, and giving them physical forms, which can be both appealing and troubling: in short, haunting.

McDowall comments on some responses to the play:

> Some people said *Pomona* was quite a cinematic play: I always thought that was just because it had a plot. When I tried breaking down why people were saying it was like a film, it seemed to me like it was just because they were excited to know what happened next; but I'd want that from anything, I don't think that's inherently cinematic.

What I care about most is story, really. Who are we following, and what do they want?

Maybe another reason it was thought to be cinematic was due to some of the reference points. I have always been obsessed with film; but I've also always been obsessed with novels, poetry, comics, music. Once I started really discovering theatre as a teenager, I was reading plays pretty much constantly, and soon got just as obsessed with writing for the stage.

I am interested in writing for the screen, but my plays are plays. At the moment I'm interested in being in a room with a story and making it explode; and the theatre is the only place I can do that. I want everyone in the room to feel it punch at the same time. Theatre's the only thing I love that disappoints me as often as it does. It's so rare to go and see a play and it's great. But what keeps me hanging on is that when you see one that *is* great, it's not just great for that evening or that week, but it's great forever, because you won't forget that feeling of being in *that room* with *that thing*. That's an event. And that's what I want to write, and I think that's a purely theatrical impulse.

(McDowall, 2016)

McDowall further suggests that shattering the stylistic "rules" of theatrical naturalism is an appropriate way to testify to the strangeness of contemporary existence: 'Real life is weird and scary, it feels technicolour and grayscale altogether. It's everything, all at once. Physicalizing that is something theatre – and only theatre – can do' (McDowall in Trueman, 2014). Interestingly, McDowall will, however, acknowledge a perceived affinity between the media of theatre and comics/graphic novels:

> A comic is two panels and a space in between; everything that happens exists in that gap. You fill in the blanks. It's the same with theatre: it's all created, not on stage or in the audience, but somewhere in the air in between them.
> (McDowall in Trueman, 2014)

This is a significant feature of *Pomona*, which challenges its audiences to "jump the gaps" imaginatively between scenes, and to reconsider earlier events from the startling perspectives of gradually emergent contexts. They have to imagine connections, in a world where *dis*connection is the rule and system of a materialistic society. Here, as Rachel Clements observes:

> disconnection takes on a broader, perhaps more political dimension. . . . There are some doors you don't want to open, Zeppo thinks. Because once you know the answer, you might have to do something different – or you might get hurt. *Pomona* is full of characters deciding whether or not to get involved, whether or not to ask questions. It's full of characters facing the gap between what they tell themselves and what they might find if they actually looked.
> (Clements, 2015)

Paul Farley and Michael Symmons Roberts have developed the term 'edgeland', first coined by Marion Shoard, as an aperture through which to reconsider 'places where an overlooked England truly exists', including 'places where the city's dirty secrets are laid bare' (Farley and Roberts, 2012: 10). These semi-forgotten, apparently no-man's-lands(capes) are where the post-industrial 'slipstream' of diverted money, energy, people and traffic has left behind 'a zone of inattention' (103), pivotal on/to the shifting borders of development, abandonment and decay. Mysterious urban and rewilding areas of dereliction, where eccentric vegetation splits and flourishes through concrete, are ruins which nevertheless contain 'a collage of time' which may threaten to 'turn space inside out' (157). These mutating wastelands indicate that 'we are only ever passing through', but they also infer that there is something discernible, however briefly, which is 'much bigger than us' (157).

McDowall's *Pomona* lends strange new flesh to these intimations, and projects recognizably urban surface processes (extending them, in a geometric sense) down into an atrocious Gothic underworld of visceral heat, oiled by self-detachment: a domain systematically malignant to human individuality, which is rendered down into disintegrated wet profit. The edgeland may appear to be 'a place of forgetting', for landfill, fly-tipping, rough sleeping: 'a place to put things out of mind on an industrial scale' (Farley and Roberts, 2012: 58–9). However, it also re-presents what might cluster at "the back of our minds", on a social and political scale: the aggression, violence and pain on which this landscape's promises and selective instances of a comfortable standard of living (for some) float, and may depend. *Pomona* offers the apocalyptically bleak vision of an everyday unconsecrated limbo, churning with a mechanized hum of industrial consumption. In *Pomona*, the mute shape of Lovecraft's Cthulhu haunts these recesses, like an edgelands' hinkypunk or neon will-o-th'-wisp, a presiding figure of terrible cosmic indifference to this human designation of human insignificance; and/or perhaps, the minotaur, to be appeased, squatting at the centre of the concrete labyrinth.

In a 2015 article for *The Guardian*, Robert McFarlane wrote about the distinctively eerie sense of the English landscape in film and literature, noting how digging 'down to reveal the hidden content of the under-earth' is a recurrent trope, and how what is discovered as the subject of this willed erasure is 'almost always a version of capital' (for example, in Patrick Keiller's 2010 film *Robinson in Ruins*, the protagonist tracks the buried cables and gas-pipes of Oxfordshire, following them as 'postmodern leylines, and tracing them outwards to hidden global structures of financial ownership'); and McFarlane adds how he eagerly awaits the English horror film 'that must surely soon be shot [featuring] sink-holes as maws' from out of which rises the demonic shape of Lovecraft's Cthulhu: 'Perhaps filming is already under way' (McFarlane, 2015). In fact, McDowall's *Pomona* was already written and staged: McFarlane was scanning the wrong medium for this manifestation of symbolic prescience.

Pomona stages this very apparition (or at the least an aptly masked devotee) stalkingly emergent from and presiding over just such an English edgeland sinkhole. On one level, this may be linked to what Chris Jenks associates with psychogeography: the initiative which aims to identify and trace 'compulsive currents within the city along with unprescribed boundaries of exclusion and unconstructed gateways of opportunity', so that 'the city begins, without fantasy or exaggeration, to take on the characteristics of a map of the mind' (Jenks, 1995: 154). However, this is also a specifically cultural and political response to contemporary crises and anxieties, as when McDowall dramatizes shockingly the systematic designation of humans' insignificance in the collateral damage of 'keeping the peace'. Indeed, the biggest impact of the discovery of oil or shale gas might not be on machinery, productivity or economies, but a fundamental transformation of how governments imply it is acceptable for people to relate to each other. When governments condone and extend the fracturing of the land's deep rock foundations, as something infinitely extendable in the name of immediate economic growth, they also accelerate an 'extraction ethic'. The principle that landscapes might be valued principally (or even exclusively) for what can be taken from them, might then be extended to people. According to this principle, the forces of "management" may, having taken what they want, thereafter appropriately discard the eviscerated husks of what was formerly natural or human, and move on (I develop this concept from an idea proposed by John O'Brien). *Pomona* stages, in hallucinatory nightmarish form, the logical implications of these ethics of government, when they (inevitably) enter social and sexual and psychological relations. Moreover, it does so without compromising its theatrical power as a wickedly funny, startlingly bizarre, unpredictably twisting, thriller-dynamic cracking yarn.

2

First loop

Let's break into hell

This chapter will identify and consider what each scene contributes to the first impressions made by the play. Scene /**one** deserves particular focus, as it is the longest scene in performance, but is intensely and insistently enigmatic in the questions it generates. It also sets up a practical challenge for the production team: how to suggest and interpret physically the initial stage directions, '*3.24 a.m./The M60 ring road./A car circles the city./ZEPPO drives. OLLIE listens.*' The limitations of realistic body language (and literalist props such as a steering wheel or car seats) will result in a static enclosure: I suggest it may be better if effects of lighting and sound evoke the setting and premise, permitting the performers a larger spectrum of body language and interactive gesture. Indeed, the third presence, '*a figure in a Cthulhu mask*', raises further questions: is this a character in the play (who will become identifiable later in the play, perhaps as Keaton) wearing a mask? Or is H. P. Lovecraft's unnerving demon Cthulhu to be portrayed as an actual character in this play? Or can this be made indeterminate?

Zeppo is eating chicken nuggets and simultaneously talking *'at a ferocious pace'* (a challenge in itself to the performer of the role, likely to involve them veering between the comic and the repulsive). Zeppo describes, with childlike exhilaration, cartoonish energy and present-tense urgency, scenes which become recognizable to Ollie, and potentially to members of the audience, as the climactic and closing scenes of Steven Spielberg's American adventure film *Raiders of the Lost Ark* (1981): a narrative which leaves final impressions poised between 'kind of a happy ending' and 'kind of a mysterious ending', because it 'makes you think, like, what's in those other boxes' in a secret laboratory warehouse (8). When Ollie points out, with careful politeness, that she knows the film (as may many), Zeppo is taken aback. Although he is a figure who commands respect, he is evidently less worldly than he may seem (or think he is). But his energy and appetite are irrepressible, if narrowly focussed: he aborts recounting the second Indiana Jones movie, and diverts into offering Ollie a 'chicken nugger' *(sic)* from the hundred he orders every night. This gleeful junk-food extravagant *largesse* is promptly shaded by Zeppo's instruction to Ollie to pass back to the mysterious Cthulhu figure behind them (a) a Rubik's cube (in the script and Ned Bennett's initial production at The Royal Welsh College of Music and Drama), or (b) a polyhedral dice, associated with role-playing games (RPGs; in all later productions and performances considered here). Why does this silent but intent figure need to be (a) occupied, distracted and appeased, or (b) involved and consulted to prompt the next initiative?

Zeppo performs hard – both frantically and disarmingly – to characterize himself to Ollie as a triumphant super-individualist. In the atomized world of the internet and iPhone, Zeppo wants to define his own story as that of an individual who is in control of his own life and feelings but also, importantly, as someone who is in touch with, and part of, how larger forces are shaping some grand picture of the future. Ollie is seeking her sister, out of concern and a sense of interdependence. However, her task is complicated by the sense that she cannot approach the police because her sister may have been involved in some things vaguely ominous, and ominously vague: what Zeppo deftly cloaks as being 'into some bad stuff' (12). Advancing a sense of his strategic '*discretion*' (12) and territorial savvy, Zeppo warns her that she is approaching the verge of a world that is not porous: it is exclusively sectioned, and properly inscrutable. He insists that, as a crucial matter of his personal code, he limits his involvement in the core matters of this world. Zeppo recalls how, when his father probed or questioned the sources of what has become Zeppo's inherited wealth, his father was killed, and made a startling example: nailed 'to a brick wall with a steel rod through his face' (13). Like many neoliberals, Zeppo masks his own privileged entitlement and fearful dismissiveness with a show of being equitable and admissive: 'So I don't get involved. I'm neutral. I'm a very neutral person. I rent my land and my buildings out to *everyone*. To *anyone*' (13); that is, anyone who can afford it, and who agrees to play the game by the enforced associated rules of the territory (Ben Piggott points out to me here that Zeppo's professed attitude has overtones of the 'True Neutral' designation in the *Dungeons & Dragons* RPG alignment system for determining characters' morality). To consolidate his own sense and performance of charismatic worldliness, Zeppo unveils his guiding principle, slickly branded as 'the most important ethos' for 'today's turbulent times': 'Selective education' (13). Again, this sounds libertarian, a range of options which offers to satisfy the consumer: 'You choose what you educate yourself about' (14). The terms on which this principle may be applied are more significant. Zeppo's gleeful adherence to brand loyalty to McDonald's products – 'Accept no substitutes' – is, he admits, momentarily complicated by an intimation of what might possibly 'turn a chicken into this' (15): a boneless parcel of pap.

These intimations are the contradiction at the core of Zeppo's character, a contradiction which makes him, dramatically, grotesquely engaging. On the one hand, he is aware that his prized top-line iPhone permits him an unprecedented rapidity of (commercially mediated) information: whereas 'twenty years ago or whatever', 'you only looked into things you cared about, cos it was *effort*' (14). On the other hand, he senses that the knowledge, potentially available to him, of the industrial processes which generate his favourite fast-food container-forms might dull his appetite, the irrepressible juvenile hedonism which constitutes his characteristic energy, which he adorns with the garish, dazzlingly cheap "bling" of his street-smart verbal assurances. Zeppo's boisterously over-whelming rhetorical zigzag is summarized in his question to Ollie: 'What do you think man? Option 1? Or B?' (15; this single-breath switchback, which demonstrates the surprising fragility of any one system of categorization, should generate audience laughter *because* of the authoritative, intent whimsical inconsistency with which Zeppo delivers it).

Zeppo presents a vividly, buoyantly imaginative argument for strategically limiting the imagination. He refuses to open the door to information which he senses might slow his pace, conscious that we are likely to find that all of our (cultural, consumer, personal) choices are built on a 'foundation of pain and shit and suffering', if we are tempted to 'go deep enough' (15). This informs his maxim: 'You can't *be* a good person any more', in a world where 'There's just people who are *aware* of the pain they're causing and people who *aren't* aware' (15). There is a potential substance and apparent seriousness to these rationalizations; as there is to Zeppo's proclamation, 'Knowledge is a *responsibility*', which permits him to "toss the shape" of philosopher-superhero to the cautiously attentive onstage audient, Ollie. However, Zeppo's interpretation and application of his "principle" of selective self-education involves him being completely unselective ('neutral') about those with whom he trades, even (especially?) when he knows them to be 'bad people'. He thinks this gives him the demi-god status of wise and (only discretely) intervening overseer ('I sit outside and I fa*cilitate*, and I *watch*'; 16), somewhere between a Marvel Comics Watcher and Dr Who (Zeppo boasts, this distantiation from human specifics and implications and consequences, when achieved, is 'like a form of time travel'). But what *exactly* does he facilitate?

Ollie, in contrast, 'can't stop thinking' about her sister, her location and what may have happened, or be happening, to her. Zeppo's sense of momentum, though extravagant, is irrelevant to Ollie's; without seeming to be rude, she admits struggling to relate his torrent of words to her sister's predicament, or her own. Zeppo's hyperactive justification for his philosophical indolence is to question whether it is, under these circumstances, a 'good idea' for Ollie to seek out her sister. Ollie's motivation is simple, direct and literally radical: 'She's my sister' (16), and a blood tie cannot be abandoned. Zeppo recoils into selective emphasis in admitting consequences: 'There are doors./And there are *doors*' (17). He disarmingly claims to like Ollie, because she offers an unusual opportunity for conversation (or, more accurately, a respectful foil for his monologues) compared to his usual petitioners, who plead predictably for money or buildings. He reveals that he nominally owns Pomona: a disused area (ironically named after a Roman goddess of fruitful abundance) which his mysterious paymasters insist he leave apparently barren, so that there is 'No reason for anyone to go there' (19). He refuses to disclose their identity, but admits that the area features in speculations about the recent disappearances of people, whilst insisting he actively does not recommend investigation. Meanwhile, the figure works on in the background and either requires placating with another Rubik's cube (having solved the puzzle of the first), or initiates the next development (scene?) with a throw of the dice.

This first scene instigates a strong sense of what David Mamet terms the hunting instinct: it sets up a quest narrative, a mysterious landscape to be investigated and the premise of separated twins, which may even recall Shakespeare's darkly romantic comedies (Ollie's name is not Viola, but probably derived from Olivia, which always makes me think of the morbidly lovelorn romantic of *Twelfth Night*, sooner than *The Comedy of Errors*). Mamet provocatively observes:

> Drama is not an attempt on the part of the dramatist to clarify, but rather to present, in its unfiltered, disturbing form, the hunt of the individual (the protagonist) such that, in its perfect form (tragedy), the end of the play reveals the folly of the hero's (and so the audience's) assumptions about the world and himself.
>
> (Mamet, 2010: 23)

Mamet later observes that in 'great drama', we recognize that freedom 'is achieved through the painful questioning of what was before supposed unquestionable' (69). These are the stakes in *Pomona*.

Scene /**two** is even more urgent and enigmatic. In a head-lit phone box, Fay, a frightened fugitive hugging a laptop, struggles with her impulses, aborts a phone call to the police and instructs her babysitter to stay on and secure the house, in terms which suggest a state of personal emergency and imminent threat. But Fay is interrupted by Keaton, whose knocking startles Fay, who barks the resonant question: 'What do you *want*?'. In response, Keaton simply 'stares' impassively and unnervingly (23).

Scene /**three** extends the premise of the desperate phone call into even stranger extremities. Gale's frustrations at being placed "on hold" by the complacent muzak labyrinth of phone banking are familiar to most of us; but here her wilful indignation takes on increasingly surreal and vengeful forms, as she tells an increasingly and unusually agitated account manager to withdraw all her account funds in cash, pile them up in the street and burn them, preferably 'in front of a food bank, or a homeless shelter' (25): a ritualistic but inexplicable nihilistic provocation, similar to the situationist 'action' allegedly practised and documented in 1994 by The K Foundation (Bill Drummond and Billy Cauty), who claimed to have burned a million pounds in cash (under circumstances detailed at https://en.wikipedia.org/wiki/K_Foundation_Burn_a_Million_Quid; accessed 22/11/2016). Gale blames the ineptness of her employees, and herself for engaging them, for this urgent if as yet essentially mysterious crisis. Then, we hear a threatening hammering on the door: this provides a counterpoint to Keaton's ominous approach to

Fay in the previous scene, but with the pressure of incursion intensified. Gale is defiant, demonstrating an edgy reckless-ness as her steady ingestion of pills prompts her to statements and actions, which are initially comic in their wildness, but become more unsettling with our gradual realization that she is trying to attain unconsciousness, even death, before her door is breached.

Scene /**four** ratchets up the stakes of the visible action still more alarmingly, as we see Moe and Charlie, dimly and intermittently lit (they are outdoors but concealed, under a bridge, '*Wet, dark, cars overhead*'; 26). Moe punches Charlie, to provoke a hurtful return blow. Moe insists these terms have to escalate, shockingly: 'it has to look real and it has to look bad' (28) if they are to avoid something even worse (raising the questions, why, and what might this be?). Char-lie's appalled reluctance and lack of fitness for this activity (he complains that hitting Moe with the force demanded has hurt his own hand) are supposed to be offset by Moe's definite (but for the audience, mysterious) narrative of rationaliza-tion ('This is the story, this is how it happened'; 'There were other people, they hurt us, she got away'; 27). Moe then intensifies matters even further by producing a knife, insisting that Charlie stab him in the side and leg, before he returns to punching and stabbing Charlie to a horrifying extent; until Charlie cries out 'Don't do any more' and questions Moe's self-control: 'You weren't going to stop' (29). Unfortunately, this does not seem to 'fix' their predicament as Moe insisted; Charlie's counter-insistence 'we messed everything up' (30) seems more pertinent, as he slides into unconsciousness, resisting the promise of an ambulance, and Moe collapses beside him, holding his hand, in the desolation of unrelenting indifference: suggested by '*Cars overhead*' (31).

This enigmatic and specifically visceral episode constitutes a further element in a sequence of startling scenes which draw the audience into the action, whilst refusing to disclose the precise terms on which they relate to each other, beyond the extreme sense of an urgent timeframe with apparent life-or-death nocturnal consequences being played out in different parts of a city.

Scene /**five** offers the audience a moment of "breathing space", by being less urgently plotted and paced. It appears to show "Ollie's" introduction, by Fay, to a place of work: a room in a brothel, where purchased physical intimacy is offered, under the surveillance of voyeuristic guards. Fay is briskly efficient, tersely discreet as she indicates the recesses of the undecorated room: a button which triggers 'you know, alarms', and a drawer which contains 'things of lube and toys and wipes' (33). In a moment of grotesque comedy, Fay also indicates that the clients may present surprising recesses of their own. "Ollie" also alludes to the fact that she is willing to undertake unusual work, including that involving 'films', to increase her pay and permit her access to 'a better sort of' drugs (36). Fay is definitely negative about her knowledge of such opportunities, and states her own and Gale's zero tolerance for drug use. It takes "Ollie's" direct question to make Fay admit the mysterious disappearances of the two previous tenants of the room.

So far into *Pomona*, McDowall is presenting direct, urgent and engaging encounters in gritty-realistic social contexts which are *almost* recognizable: conceivable, but thankfully outside the reach of most first-hand lived experience, yet gradually apparent as being subject to unusual rules. The play incorporates familiar contemporary details, often reflecting the contested issues of security and surveillance: iPhone, laptops, security cameras. McDowall is also inviting us to pay attention to these habitually familiar elements in the world by 'making them strange', rendering them *un*familiar through unexpected juxtapositions and framings. This is a form of *Verfremdungseffekt*, or estrangement, which is often associated with the political theatre of Bertolt Brecht (and in which context it is usually unhelpfully translated as "the alienation effect"), directing our attention to 'what happens between people', not just 'what happens to them' (Davis, 2016: 48). David Edgar offers another widely applicable model of estrangement, as 'a form of stimulus' which invites and allows us to recognize 'the oddness of things' as 'the first step in freeing ourselves from that day-to-day numbing down of our perceptions which sees the status quo as natural and inevitable'; furthermore, 'Brecht wanted to estrange the world's doings so that we would be prodded into asking how they fitted into a pattern obscured by rhetoric, sentiment and familiarity' (Edgar, 2009: 19; terms of objective and technique which are identifiable in the work of McDowall and other contemporary dramatists, such as Rudkin, Bond, Barker, Kane, Butterworth and green). Edgar further observes that plays which

> put together two or three apparently unrelated narratives and invite the audience to connect them – as happens in three of Sarah Kane's five plays – imply or even insist that making cause-and-effect connections is harder than it used to be, but they also assert the overwhelming human urge to do so.
>
> (115)

Edgar gives the example of Ravenhill's *Shopping and Fucking*, but one might also cite Simon Stephens's *Pornography* (2007), the entire work of Samuel Beckett, and *Pomona*.

In *Pomona*, McDowall is furthermore distinctively adding elements of the thriller or *film noir*: he incorporates the motif of mysteriously disappearing girls, sets up a taut timeframe in which the characters feel pressured to avoid, appease or perform gangland violence (examples of specifically British film thrillers might be Mike Hodges's *Get Carter*, 1971, or Guy Ritchie's *Lock, Stock and Two Smoking Barrels*, 1998). McDowall has stated, in *Pomona* 'I wanted the audience to become the detective within the play, accruing information', in order to assemble it into deductive meaning; 'and as they did so, they would feel as though they were being pulled down further and further underground' (McDowall, 2016), into a deeper and more disturbing sense of possible consequences. Kate Tempest's novel, *The Bricks That Built the Houses* (2016), similarly starts by evoking a distinctly contemporary version of the generic world and fast pace of the urban thriller, depicting characters who survive or advance precariously, edging into a predatory underworld. Like McDowall, Tempest subsequently builds narrative pressure, curiosity and excitement whilst also developing characters to (genre-subverting) points where they prove to be surprisingly, unpredictably engaging and complex. However, McDowall will moreover develop his fictional *landscape* of Pomona, as well as his characters, into astonishing depths.

Scene /**six** initially appears to lighten the mood, with what promises to be a less brooding encounter. Keaton presents herself at a club meeting convened by Charlie, for those potentially interested in *Dungeons & Dragons* and other RPGs. Charlie's excitement at inducting her into his restricted field of "mastery" is tinged with bathos, as we learn that Keaton is the only respondent so far, to invitations for meetings now in their fourth week. Charlie is childlike in his eagerness, which veers into potential prying abruptness: 'Sorry, I'm being rude' (38). He is also both comically endearing and pathetic in his manifest loneliness, and his exhilaration at her striking if strange presence, her expensive if eccentric clothes (her two-hundred-pound trainers, and perhaps headphones, which she wears without fear or consideration of theft). Keaton is differently and enigmatically abrupt, possibly seeming as if she may have some autism spectrum disorder: she is intensely focussed, but she limits her forms of interaction in repetitive ways. If Charlie's admission that he has only one friend, 'through work', is pitiful (particularly if we connect this with Moe, whom we have witnessed beating and stabbing Charlie in another context), Keaton's blunt indication that she has no friends at all extends her eccentricity further. However, this does not unnerve Charlie, but increases his puppy dog exuberance: he assures her 'we're gonna make friends now', enthusing how RPGs offer 'a very social experience./Even though there's only two of us' (40). After offering her lemonade and crisps, Charlie proudly introduces his own invented game, 'Cthulhu Awakens', based on Lovecraft's mythos of the supernatural 'Great Old Ones' – 'They're actually sort of a metaphor for the universe's apathy for us and the meaningless nature of life' – and a bid to thwart a cult who are trying to awaken Cthulhu to 'begin a new dark reign of chaos' (41).

Keaton's agreement to start the game leads (or cues) scene /**six** to bleed into scene /**seven**: the first scenario in Charlie's game takes place on 'a crowded street' in a 'cold and lonely city', with the objective, 'to search for your sister' who has 'disappeared under mysterious circumstances' (42). And indeed, Charlie and Keaton's merging recitations of details joins with that of Ollie, almost like an incantation, as Ollie, in some unspecified unshared reality, appears to enact or reflect the choices in narrative (re)action. While Charlie and Keaton remain intent on their game, Ollie enacts walking a circuit through the city, amidst numbed pedestrians who seem to have surrendered significant consciousness to the tramlines of economic determinism, which transport them through a series of effects and products rather than causes ('It's hard to recognise when your life is looping'; 42). Charlie and Keaton's narration of their "game" incorporates further details which reflect Ollie's odyssey, such as 'the man in the car' on the road around the city, and the 'hole' at the city's heart (43). However, on the 'maybe/eighth' loop of soporific trudging through a shopping centre, the 'horror' and 'terror' of a woman becomes detectable: notably, she alone has purchased nothing, but clutches a laptop, and looks as if 'she's just seen/the face of God/or some unimaginable sight' (44). The robotic shoppers surprisingly assist Ollie, defending her from this apparent sad screaming city derelict, who then disappears, as if absorbed, or like a 'ghost' (46). Then the crowd resumes its rhythm of movement and non-thought: but Ollie proclaims her own 'flow of looping and thinking' broken, which prompts her sudden 'frozen' but distinctive recognition of how, all around her, other people's looping resumes, assimilating this fracture (47).

Scene /**eight** skilfully releases tension by featuring *Pomona*'s most outrageously comic moments, as Charlie passes his time at work with Moe; then the scene re-escalates tension through Gale's arrival with new orders and a threat. Charlie's childlike openness makes him a vulnerable out-of-depth player in this predatory world, whereas Moe prides himself on being the harder, senior, strategic half of what Gale calls their 'double act'. However, Moe finds himself rendered (comically) uneasy by the frankness and extravagance with which Charlie elaborates on the topics of his urges, his formative sexual experiences and fantasies: the audience are also likely to be surprised, and perhaps shocked, by that at which they find (and hear) that they can laugh. Charlie extrapolates from conducting his playground game with his own saliva, to recalling another (avowedly non-sexual) impulse to bestow his semen on everything and everyone ('Even you', he tells a startled Moe). He then reminisces about his favourite childhood site (and method) for masturbation, and his glimpses of patients in a neighbouring hospital. The more Moe tries to curtail Charlie's reflections on the possible resonances of these details, the further Charlie persists; his final observation, 'I think probably Freud would have something to say about it' (50), is a laughable understatement after such baroque carnality. Gale is, on immediate arrival, brusque and (dark-comically) mean in her impatience with Charlie, but her hastening tempo, murderous assignment and intensifying threats all counter the momentum of his misplaced enthusiasm. However, it is not the threat of blinding that finally unnerves Charlie, but Gale's ominous invocation of 'The Girl'. Though Moe tries to maintain that assassinations are not what he and Charlie 'really do', Gale reminds them that they are paid more than would be expected, merely to guard a security gate. Moe's ultimate order to Charlie, to pick up the crumpled paper with the details of their human target, has the contractual effect of accepting a summons, though it is significantly passed further down the hierarchical chain of command.

Scene /**nine** (which picks up from the narrative events of /**five**, and perhaps /**seven**, several days or weeks later)

initially returns us from gangland *noir* to the grim social real-
ism of the prostitutes' world, where the rules of behaviour
are also fundamentally determined in financial terms, voyeuristically patrolled and forcibly imposed. Indeed, the scene
opens up further abominable extensions of these principles,
as we learn that "Ollie" has become embroiled in a hard-
core sex film involving her in actual beating and forced sex.
She initially tries to explain away her injuries as the effect
of a mugging, but Fay points out that these will debar her
from her standard trade, at least temporarily. Fay's fussy
(wilful?) naïvety gives way to realization of the depths to which
"Ollie" has gone, for the double bind of payment (that is
'not enough') for (drug-related?) debts which are 'too much
to pay back' (59). "Ollie's" words skate hesitantly, euphe-
mistically around the depths of horror, trying to contain
what should not be contained: 'It was like a rape −/A rape
thing./That was the story. Of the film'; in response, Fay's
exclamation, 'Oh' (58), signifies a collapse of words. "Ollie"
then unfolds two semi-hallucinogenic reveries: first, that she
'thinks' or 'feels like' she has a twin sister, named Ollie, who
may be looking for her, and which may somehow account for
"Ollie's" sensation that 'I can remember seeing myself places
I haven't been to' (60). Second, "Ollie's" righteously violent
anger at Fay's policeman husband, and all abusive and hypo-
critical men, leads her into a nihilistic soliloquy in which she
projects her own apotheosis as a flaming angel of destructive
vengeance. "Ollie" also administers the stern warning that,
should she disappear, she is nevertheless not to be sought.
This overt acknowledgment of an identical twin/*doppelgänger*
to the protagonist should make audience members question
their interpretation of preceding events and scenes, even as it
opens up further nightmarish senses of possibility.

Scene /**ten** picks up from scene /**eight**, and depicts
Charlie and Moe reflecting on their assignment and situation. Charlie's playing with 'Pokemons' (*sic*) on a Gameboy
emphasizes his childish aspect, even as it evokes a kitsch cartoon setting for captured monsters who are trained to fight
each other. However, though Charlie identifies himself as
usually good at not thinking about things, he cannot keep
at bay his own concern at their orders to murder, or his fear
of 'The Girl', the portent who presages death: who does
not personally cause a death, but decrees its means. Moe
insists that there have to be 'reasons' to inform their lethal
mission, their intended victim must have done something
to deserve it. However, Charlie counters with the personal
testimony that refutes this notional justice: Charlie cannot
find any employment other than this, because he has a crim-
inal record; he went to jail, not for perpetrating any harm-
ful action, but for association with a murderous schoolboy
friend who went on a shooting spree. Charlie's physical
proximity to the schoolboy, their friendship and the 'angry
stuff' he wrote in a personal notebook were sufficient evidence to convict him. This sudden dilation of Charlie's character gives his arrested development (and continued search
for trust and friendship) additional pathos. He is also (not
always inappropriately) childlike in his insistence on asking
questions of the bewildering "adult" world around him, its
rules and secrets: for example, what is contained in the vans,
which pass through the gates which they guard, into the tunnels beneath the Pomona district of Manchester? Moe hesitantly replies to Charlie's demands that he must at least have
a theory about this; Moe's question, 'Do you know what a
snuff film is?' (72), is left to hang in the air of their silence,
and that of the audience.

Scene /**eleven** returns the focus to the brothel, where Fay confronts Gale, demanding to know the whereabouts of Ollie's twin. Gale is sufficiently startled by Fay's presence in Gale's office, '*clutching a laptop*', for this to constitute a stand-off: Gale tries to undermine Fay's self-belief, taunting her for concern about her more autonomous 'little friend' and for her repeated patterns of self-subjugation ('Just because you've *nailed* yourself to that bed, doesn't mean others – '; 74). Fay has another important question which Gale finds unanswerable: why does Gale have the blood types of her girls, "disappeared" and present, stored on her laptop? Gale mocks Fay's concern and involvement as forms of repeatedly craving pain and misery, but Fay overcomes this vicious account of her cyclical susceptibility to victimhood, and insists she is leaving with the laptop; though Gale successfully undercuts Fay's initial, conventional threat to take it to the police, because this will only return her to the sphere of her abusive husband's social authority. Gale tries further to activate Fay's insecurity, threatening her with mysterious 'people' who will find her, wherever she goes. The scene ends, tensely poised in the second before whatever Fay's decisive action may be.

Surprisingly, scene /**twelve** initially appears to offer some light relief by returning us to Charlie's role-playing game with Keaton, begun in scene /**six**. Charlie's invented game is vividly, if geekishly, confined to his rather formulaically melodramatic elaboration of motifs from Lovecraft's Cthulhu mythos. Keaton, always (and sometimes unnervingly) intent, seems keenly absorbed: Charlie alternates between offering her sympathetic hints and encouraging comments, surprised by her skill, and assuming the characters of her adversaries with over-ripe hubristic statements of self-conscious evil, reminiscent of Dr Strange's cosmic opponents. The momentum of Keaton's involvement in the game is then punctured by Charlie's bathetic need to urinate, taking him thoroughly out of role, as does his return – after what may and should be something at least close to a real-time hiatus – with the childlike gift of lemonade for them to share. Keaton is not resistant, but remains wilful, refusing to use her weapons in the game as often as Charlie suggests. Charlie's gauche bid to propose a date ('to watch a film or something') to cement and develop their friendship is bluntly quashed by Keaton ('I can't'); Charlie resigns himself to returning to his work as a security guard. This information, however, piques Keaton's abrupt interest, and Charlie tells her how he and Moe guard a gate in the unstable landscape of Pomona: through which vans, carrying something he suspects to be illegal, disappear into labyrinthine subterranean tunnels, possibly leading to some warehouse-like edifice. Keaton has an insistent emotional reaction to this information, telling Charlie 'You shouldn't work there', but withholding any specific reason why not (83); she wants to abort the train of conversation and return to the terms of the game, urgently.

Charlie complies, donning a home-made Cthulhu mask in order to assist his return to an adversarial speaking role. In production, Charlie's donning of his home-made Cthulhu mask initiates a sequence in which he becomes more animated, his movements more menacing, and the scene's lighting may become more ominous (as it did in Ned Bennett's production), reflecting and amplifying the sense of the character's associations and the game's more serious issues – cosmic moral indifference, slavery on a global scale, human sacrifice – and their reverberations, from the immediate to the uncanny (in our Aberystwyth production, the separate form of our Cthulhu figure was a dimly emergent and briefly visible presence, watching wryly from the shadows as Charlie performed his manifestation). This mood, however, is also punctured, by the promptings of Keaton's mobile phone, meaning that, as she simply says, she has to go, now. Charlie's expression of hope for a future continuation of their game and contact goes unanswered.

Scene /**thirteen** appears to sidestep from any readily identifiable point in the narrative timeline, depicting Moe's visit to the brothel, where he encounters Fay. She is tersely professional, as when she introduced "Ollie" (and the audience) to the meeting room in scene /**five**, but this time Fay is operating in the formal situation of transactional sex. McDowall's finely tuned ear for rhythmic writing is at its best in this scene, with its carefully arranged ' . . . ' ellipses (which the script specifies should indicate 'either a trailing off, a breather, a shift, or a transition'; 6) punctuating initiatives, hesitations and disclosures. The stage directions' specification that Moe seat himself '*as far away as he can*' from Fay adds further dramatic artistry, ensuring that the stage picture avoids the literalness of televisual or cinematic proxemics in suggesting intimacy, but rather opening up a distinctly theatrical spatial relationship between the performers, so that the audience have to choose where to look, across a space in which the spoken words can hang (like cigarette smoke or trickling fireworks), and in which the heat of speculative performative interaction can be conducted. Fay's defensive indication of 'security' on Moe's first mention of the word 'Violence' (87) may effectively indicate the audience, standing in for the unseen security guards who voyeuristically follow the transactions of apparent intimacy through monitors. Moe works, firmly if stammeringly, to slow Fay's fluent pace towards conventional foreclosures, by insisting he does not want what

she thinks he wants: rather than sex, he wants to talk, and he
deliberately sets his chair '*as far away as he can*' from her (85).
Fay is nonplussed, maintaining that, unlike sex, 'You can't
buy conversation' about 'Personal things' (86). Moe's conventional icebreaker, 'Is this a good place to work?', draws
her impatient contempt: 'Of course it's not', because she
has 'to have sex with people for money' (86). Nevertheless,
Fay, maintaining that she is unshockable and has the right
to refuse, tries to accelerate the transaction to the "bottom
line" of whatever Moe might want. His admission that he
just wants to touch her is nevertheless distinguished by him
from being 'a, a sex thing' (87), a fetishistic means to cli-
max, but rather an occasion for something from which he
has been separated by his 'issues with, uh –/Violence / . . . '
(87). His admission of this, and acceptance of Fay's identifi-
cations of his former actions as 'disgusting' and 'awful', do
not provoke her sympathy. She does divulge that she and
her daughter were hurt by her husband, confirming for her
that the 'whole world hates women' (91), a proposition that
Moe considers thoroughly: 'Maybe. Not me. I don't think'
(91). Fay has already admitted that she does not find Moe
to be like her husband: 'You're quiet' (90), and her gener-
alization about men – though evidently a deduction from
bruising experience – seems partly to be set up with the possibility of its being contested. Her further challenge to Moe –
'You think you're different from other men' (91) – draws
his simple admission of a wish, not for death, but the release
from the hazards of interaction: an 'amazing kind of peace'
(92). In response (and recognition?), Fay removes her shoe
and '*very slowly stretches her leg across the gap between them*' (92);
breathlessly, Moe reaches across to hold her foot. Thus, they
both demonstrate an ability to diverge from the determinism

of their expected (and even characteristic) behaviour, significantly expanding the sense of prevalent sense of human possibility with these actions.

Scene /**fourteen** is a wordless interlude which takes place predominantly in darkness, depicting Ollie's flashlit progression '*underground*', through a tunnel. It provides the audience with an intensified and startling experience of seeing and knowing no more than the character(s) can, rendering the performance space surprisingly fluid through light, and perhaps hinting at further disclosures (examples of staging this scene are provided in the next section).

Scene /**fifteen** follows on some brief time after scene /**eleven** (but before scenes /**two** and /**eight**): it depicts Gale forced to admit to Keaton that Fay '*has* −/Left', taking the laptop, but seeking to assure Keaton that the 'two men' which Gale "has" are 'good' enough to rectify the unforeseen hitch (94), though Gale acknowledges that Keaton may prefer to intervene, decisively and lethally, herself (95). Keaton's silence drives Gale to lower her own status, uncharacteristically, even further ('It's my mess./I'll clean it up./Of course.'; 95). Keaton then reveals the abominable depths of the central process, in which Gale is complicit, and how they outstrip even Gale's supposition that the 'girls' she 'gives' the unseen operatives might be used, lethally, to make snuff films. The processes of organ harvesting and forcible impregnation for baby farming provide nightmarish glimpses of ultimate forms of systematic objectification and violation of human beings for more highly valued financial profit. Keaton's threat, that Gale will be a particularly promising subject for an intensified Procrustean version of the process, is delivered with a childlike detachment ('I'll tell them to put a baby in you'; 97), as if Keaton is a child visiting her wilful cruelty on a doll, indeed threatening to reduce Gale to a doll: attractive enough to be hollow(ed out). Her final insistence (not a question) – 'Do you see.' (98) – challenges both Gale and the audience to manage imaginatively the ramifications of what has been revealed.

Scene /**sixteen** leads into the immediate consequences of Gale's bid to 'clean it up', showing how Moe and Charlie have captured Fay, in accordance with the assignment given them in scene /**eight** and considered further by them in scene /**ten**. However, neither Moe and Charlie nor Fay has the all-important laptop containing the incriminating records of the "disappeared" women, a crucial element in Gale's assignment. The full context and resonances of this tense opening tableau will become increasingly apparent: the bound, kneeling figure with a zipped rucksack on her head may appear initially slightly ludicrous as well as pathetic, and perhaps only then recognizable as Fay. Tellingly, Charlie objects that, rather than anonymizing or objectifying their victim, 'The bag makes it worse' (99) because of how it throws into relief her desperate breathing, as well as preventing clear responses to their questions. However, Moe insists that the bag should stay on: that 'Everything bad is real' (101); her involvement, and theirs, and the consequent situation is inevitable. Charlie decisively challenges this determinism, in his own stumbling but heartfelt way: 'We don't *know* that', or even what they are 'involved *in*'; crucially, in a world of broken promises, Charlie breaks rank and decides to be his own example: 'I keep thinking that everything will get better but it doesn't, it just gets worse, and if I do this then it'll be even worse than that' (100). However naïvely, Charlie expresses a form of heroism in his attempt to be a 'good person'.

This in turn challenges Moe's armoured cynicism, which even Charlie thinks is intrinsic to his sole friend ('You don't care about anything'; 101). Crucially, Moe admits that his habitual motivation by self-hatred ('Why would I want to live in a world that would let me walk on it?'; 102) has splintered on the discovery of his own wish, that Charlie's simple attempt to be good should not require his death. This sudden dilation of Moe's character, this howling but decisive breaking *open*, presages further startling vulnerabilities: Charlie's removal of the bag from Fay's head means that, though gagged, she can meet Moe's eyes, and he hers, before she escapes. So the fragile subterfuges of pretended anonymity are dispelled: Fay knows the identities of her abductors; more personally, she will recognize her principal attacker as the man she conceded might be 'different' to her abusive ex-husband when she encountered Moe as a client in the brothel (in scene /**thirteen**). Having met her gaze, Moe cannot bring himself to block her escape. After a '*Pause*', he decisively, if bizarrely, instructs Charlie 'Hit me' (103), and cues the narrative to plunge into the (now, recontextualized, even more appalling) sequence previously established, elaborated and witnessed in scene /**four**.

Scene /**seventeen** follows Ollie's flashlit odyssey '*deeper into the tunnels*' (104), and surrounds her with the dimly visible forms of all other characters, in unshared terms of reality. As in the mall scene, /**seven**, Ollie expresses and enacts her choices in reaction whilst the others roll dice, and develop narrative premises and contexts as in a role-playing game. Her narrated route takes her through the cracked concrete, tall grass and down into enigmatic cable tunnels which can be observed and negotiated in the actual Manchester district of Pomona; then further, past a locked steel door and mysterious operatives. It is as if Ollie has penetrated the nightmare world produced by the waking but drifting "sleep" of conformity in a "reason" governed by and appealing to financial transactions which depend on a complete and inimical indifference to human variety and value. The troubling nature of her discoveries of rows of young men and pregnant women, secured and sutured in institutional beds, may be extended if the production directs the performers to situate what they identify within the audience's seating area, effectively "casting" the audience as the drugged, slumbering and systematically evacuated throngs. Still seeking her sister, Ollie stumbles across the full inventory of this hellish world, from plastic cradle to plastic tubs of cremated ash, as the pace, stakes and urgency of the scene increase relentlessly. In the increasingly gothic imagery of condensed and extreme nightmare logic, Ollie and the audience are directed to "see", from a hiding point under a bed, a new female inmate, undressed and strapped down by men, before Ollie herself feels a hand around her ankle, pulling her out into their predatory view, with the final fearful intimation that death may be preferable to life now she is discovered.

Scene /**eighteen** takes an artful sidestep into bewildering, surreal comedy, depicting Charlie – now dead – '*flying high over the city*', encountering Zeppo (in his first appearance since scene /**one**), now transformed somehow into '*a seagull*' (110). After the increasingly claustrophobic heat of the last scene, the sudden airy release (reincarnation?) of these characters is a relief, but also begs further questions as to their terms of their new sensations of freedom (if indeed it is). Zeppo is breezily indifferent to Charlie's disorientation, intent on his own avian mission – as gleeful, abject and childish as ever – to cover everyone and everything in the city in his shit. Charlie's impressed reiteration of his own impulse, to cover everyone and everything in semen as an act of beneficence, is dismissed by Zeppo as contrastingly 'weird' (111). On reflection, Charlie is frustrated by this irrevocable interruption of his unfinished, and now unfinishable, game with 'this girl', Keaton. Zeppo reveals a startling demonic knowledge of Charlie's past encounters, cynically maintaining that he and Moe should have killed Fay, 'You'd all be better off' (112; begging the question: how, exactly?), and insisting Charlie was 'glad' when his homicidal school friend shot two other pupils. Charlie does not answer, assimilating his own sudden vantage point of distance from humanity, which makes them look 'so small'; Zeppo remains dismissive, refuting individual significance ('They are small [. . .] They're nothing'; 112).

Scene /**nineteen** returns us to the perspective of these figures, on, and emergent from, the ground. In Pomona, "Ollie", in a hospital gown, stumbling '*aimlessly*', encounters Keaton. "Ollie"'s gown and fragmentary narrative will make it increasingly evident to the audience (now, if not beforehand) that a single female performer is portraying both Ollie and Ollie's Twin; and that the release of the latter appears to be the result of the self-sacrifice of the former (another appalling gradual realization).

"Ollie" relates how she has surfaced through a hatch in the ground, and pieces together fragmentary impressions of being awakened in a hospital bed, pulled by a hand on her leg 'out of my sleep and into the light' (113); and how another woman was being pulled out from under a bed, during which she escaped. Keaton is characteristically unmoved, demonstrating no shock or curiosity about the revelation of the many people underground which "Ollie" offers to show her. Ascertaining Keaton's name, "Ollie" realizes she does not recollect her own. Keaton is considering her own discovery:

'My friend is dead' (114). She has discovered Charlie's body under the bridge which dominates one end of Pomona, and feels unfamiliar pains of disconnection: partly from the realization that their game of 'Cthulhu Awakens' cannot be completed, so she 'won't know how the story ends now', how she has to defeat the 'great evil force' that has awoken (114); but moreover, the once unnervingly friendless Keaton registers and acknowledges a sadness in realizing that her first and only 'friend' Charlie is dead. "Ollie" responds with her own sense of isolation and loss, the intimation that she thinks she has a sister, whom she has lost, and who will now be in trouble.

In response to "Ollie"'s request for advice in finding out where the missing sister might be, Keaton suggests she wait, at night, on the road orbiting the city, till she encounters the man who drives around it all night, who owns most of the city: a verbal motif which has the ritualistic effect of a litany, invoking the opening scene of the play. They both absorb the silence of the Pomona landscape, broken only by distant cars. The usually impassive Keaton expresses a unique flash of interventionist rage, an impulse to 'burn it all down', 'to nothing', but the accompanying suspicion that 'they'd only start again' (116): an apparently nihilistic outburst of destruction may be trumped by a more profoundly nihilistic sense that nothing would change, and that current reflexes would reassert themselves. "Ollie" smiles at her, as if in dim recollection of her own similar fantasy of destructive apotheosis in scene /**nine**.

The published script directs Keaton, then "Ollie", then all other characters to pick up and begin solving a Rubik's cube, then leave the stage when their cube is solved. However, for Ned Bennett's production at The Orange Tree (and his subsequent production of *Pomona* at the Royal National Theatre Studio and Manchester Royal Exchange), the motif of the cube had been replaced by the motif of RPG dice, thrown by all the characters, here also (a decision preferred for, and incorporated into, our Aberystwyth production). The incorporation of the dice-throwing motifs into *Pomona* does not, admittedly, determine the (re)direction of the play's scripted plot. But it indicates a positive faith in something other than human patterns of conformity in predictability, as a basis for an existential commitment to choices made, and to their consequences.

If Ollie has indeed sacrificed herself to save her Twin, *Pomona* stands poised, with tragic grace: we should not despair, because one of the twins is saved; we should not presume, because one of the twins is damned. It's a reasonable percentage.

Alone on stage, "Ollie" again listens to and remarks on the quietness of the edgeland: then summons the focus to embark decisively on some unspoken (unknown? unspeakable?) initiative, which will take her beyond it.

So now: let us, similarly, go back, *and* beyond. . . .

3

Second loop
The double act of you

You start with a story in the simplest way possible, by asking, what do these characters want? And eventually you should get to the point where you ask, what does this *play* want? What is the engine of it trying to do with the audience? Is it attacking them? Seducing them? What?

(McDowall, 2016)

I now want to identify some of the connections and echoes which may become apparent on a second viewing, reading or consideration of the ways that the scenes of *Pomona* unfold. This involves attention to the actively creative processes which the audience may bring to bear on the drama. As Ken Robinson has observed, a play in performance is catalytic, not something an audience can 'unravel systematically by reading off its meaning like a computer print out'; rather:

Like the actors and director, the audience is involved in interpreting what it sees. A play is open to interpretation on two levels: what is expressed in the play and what is expressed by the play. We interpret what is being expressed in the play as it unfolds before us, by following piecemeal the actions of the characters. It is only when that play is over that we can make sense of the play as a whole.

(Robinson, 2011: 193)

This is particularly pertinent to *Pomona*, which challenges and encourages its audience to imagine what may lie beyond the doors it opens: to consider causes, in contradiction of Zeppo's exclusive focus on products and effects.

In scene /**one**, Zeppo resembles one of the vain fantastic beasts Lewis Carroll's Alice encounters in her adventures in Wonderland, or Through the Looking Glass. He is not fully attuned (or attentive) to the urgency of this young stranger's concerns, but cheerfully and extensively delineates the somewhat hallucinogenic intricacy of a world which proceeds by reference to a nebulous order which is quite alien, perhaps even inscrutable, to her.

We may note how Ollie has compulsive nightmares about what may be happening to her sister, but wakes with her own body cut and clawed, possibly by herself. Rather than the displacement and distantiation practised and expounded by Zeppo, Ollie suffers from uncontrollable collapses between fantasy and reality. Zeppo's image of the '*doors*' which, once opened, prove irrevocable, suggests entwined danger and provocation, like Pandora's Box. This in turn reminds me of the 1955 *film noir* by Robert Aldrich, *Kiss Me Deadly*, the story and style of which apparently begin in hard-boiled detective form, then burgeon startlingly into apocalyptic, and apparently nihilistic, science fiction, in an extrapolation of social anxiety and paranoia. Aldrich's film also features a fugitive female escapee from an asylum, who is fatefully given a

lift in a car, and another disingenuous waif-like female figure, who apparently works in support of an evil scientist, but
who climactically decides to trigger all-encompassing nuclear
destruction, on personal impulse.

Zeppo's nightly gorgings and infantilism suggest that he
may be the client to whom Fay refers in Scene Five, the
man who presented himself with a piece of chicken lodged in
his intimate parts. Zeppo prides himself on being a survivor,
watcher and facilitator; in hindsight, his activities constitute
just another loop, maintaining a determined superficiality
in his materialism and indifference. However, the troubling
story of his father's disfigurement in death stages the break-
down of the myth of cosmopolitan metropolitan access in the
face of its unscripted Hyde-shadow: brutal violence.

Zeppo's name corresponds with that of the sometime
Marx Brother, positioned as the "straight man" to his sib-
lings' madcap antics. Zeppo Marx played characters who
performed the role of, and apparently thought of themselves
as, the heroic romantic lead: characters who were blankly
accepting of the undercutting absurdity raging around them,
and who blithely assisted the most conventional events in the
story to progress.

The goddess Pomona's traditional attribute of the prun-
ing knife, and her association with fruitful abundance, gain
darkly ironic, nightmarishly ominous resonances in the context of the play's subsequent disclosures: harvesting of human
organs and forceful impregnations.

In retrospect, scene /**two** appears to take place after the
events of scenes /**seven** and /**fifteen**, maybe even /**nineteen**.
The laptop which Fay holds is the one she has taken from
Gale in /**eleven**, and the confrontation in /**two** may seem
to bear out Gale's threat to Fay that it 'Doesn't matter about

police./Doesn't matter how far you run': 'They find every-body' (78). Despite her pathetic attempts at altruism, these may be the last moments in Fay's story, as Keaton might carry out her orders, or unleash an undiscriminating torrent of destruction. However, Keaton *might* not. She might sim-ply have something to tell Fay. You decide.

The events of scene /**three** take place after those of scene /**fifteen**. Gale has evidently failed to 'fix' the situation of Fay's escape with the laptop, and the mysterious 'they' to whom Keaton refers in scene /**fifteen** have come to 'take' her. Oddly, this is Gale's most sympathetic scene: we can appreciate in retrospect that she is defying her superiors for once, and attempting to spare herself the awfully extended fate with which Keaton has threatened her, by placing herself beyond their reach. McDowall has commented on Gale, the comic elements of her (self-)limitations and exasperation:

> Gale seems solely driven by money, and I thought that was interesting because usually a character who seems that way will later say 'of course this is all because of my ter-rible childhood' or similar, but it's interesting if we don't have any of that, and that somehow you still feel some small amount of sympathy for her, maybe because she's just quite funny in how cruel she is, or because she ends up in such an extreme situation that you can't help but hope she makes it out, despite all the horror she's been a part of inflicting. It was interesting to see if you could feel for characters you normally wouldn't, without giving explanation as to their action. If I just ramped the stakes up so high, so you felt I don't want *any* of these characters to face such an awful fate.

Character is always best revealed through action. You learn more about Charlie watching him set up the game for Keaton than you do when he tells us what happened to him when he was younger.

(McDowall, 2016)

Scene /**four** reveals character through action in even more striking terms, by suggesting the different characters and the working relationship of Moe and Charlie, even as they struggle to overcome whatever terms of care or interaction might usually prevail between them, and perform a demonstrative violence on each other's bodies. Charlie and Moe evidently have a relationship based on some degree of co-operative trust, now itself transformed into a matter of jeopardy: the exchange may initially seem reminiscent of a sado-masochistic sexual encounter which tips out of consenting control, but increasingly resembles that of two Roman gladiators, struggling to overcome immediate fellow feeling, wounding each other more and more appallingly in some obscure offering to unseen superiors.

In retrospect, scenes /**two**, /**three** and /**four** all introduce the audience to characters (Fay, Gale, Charlie and perhaps Moe) at what seems likely to be the end of their respective "stories". Ironically, the first actions we see them perform may be the last actions they are able to perform (thanks to Patrick Young for this observation). The episodic, non-linear narrative of the play is building up suspense, not so much through conventional anticipation – as it is becoming increasingly difficult to anticipate what the next episode might comprise – as through curiosity (what are the terms of the developmental process at work for characters and play?), allied to emotional engagement with the characters. McDowall writes deftly and wittily to create footholds for this: though we may be puzzling over what the overall "journeys" of the characters (and us, the audience) may comprise, we are likely to find much that is theatrically compelling: Zeppo's zanily elevated performance of his professed identity as wacky philosopher-king, Ollie's overlaying a self-lacerating concern with (slightly impatient) attempts at polite respect, Fay's divided but intense concerns, Gale's scorchingly destructive impatience, Moe's attempt to construct a strategy out of imperfectly focussed violence, Charlie's shock as the terms of his trust in Moe are broken, along with the limits of his own physical body. If scene /**one** is initially amusing, it becomes increasingly ominous, and, like scenes /**two**, /**three** and /**four**, brings us to a brink of both *terror*, where a darkly obscured object is externalized and limits reconstituted, and *horror*, a moment of contraction in response to an excess that cannot be transcended, which in turn 'signals a temporality that cannot be recuperated by the mortal subject' (Botting, 1996: 9, 10, 75): a point of no return. They are also likely to demonstrate how terror may provoke an uneasy laughter, provoked by the startling collapse of supposedly stable boundaries and categories.

The events of scene /**five** may, on reflection, be the earliest in a linear chronology of the play's events, as well as introducing McDowall's artful running effect of theatrical *trompe l'œil*: it is only at the end of the script of *Pomona* that the reader encounters his specification:

> The actor playing Ollie plays two characters.
> In scenes One, Seven, Fourteen and Seventeen she plays Ollie.
> In scenes Five, Nine and Nineteen she plays Ollie's twin sister (118).

Hence my inverted commas around the script's given character name of "Ollie", where appropriate, in my 'First Loop' section. Whilst we are informed of this more confident twin who is into some 'bad stuff', the point of realization, that this is our first theatrical glimpse of her, is left to the individual audience member. However, those involved in production may well choose to incorporate a "depth charge": some observable, subtle, if intrinsically unremarkable, clue to distinction, which subsequently proves explosive. Ned Bennett's production chose to give Ollie's Twin a slightly eccentric red hat; in our Aberystwyth production, Rose Robinson, the performer of Ollie, removed her own habitually worn spectacles to perform Ollie's Twin, but retained them to play Ollie: a discrimination both significant and practical, within the fiction of the play.

Scene /**five** introduces Ollie's Twin and depicts her "point of departure" in the play, perhaps some time chronologically earlier than Ollie's enquiries in scene /**one**. It also depicts the (addicted?) desperation that is specific to Ollie's Twin, and her willingness to push the boundaries of all around her, even those of Fay and Gale.

Scene /**six** also belongs, in a Newtonian linear chronology, before scenes /**one** to /**four**. This presents Charlie's first (and only?) encounter with Keaton (who he may or may not subsequently associate with the figure of 'The Girl': if so, this gives specifically urgent reasons for his anxiety in scene /**eight**; if not, it demonstrates his openness, perhaps his naïvety). The playing of the scene is likely to generate some comic engagement with Charlie, both pathetic and endearing in his childishly accelerating bid to befriend this striking young woman, even as her impassiveness raises questions as to her motives and agenda. Charlie's emphasis is significant: that his invented game is not a competitive game, in which Keaton has to 'beat' him, but a co-operative game, 'in the sense that I tell the story and present you with options, and you decide which options to take', with the success of the outcomes determined by the rolling of polyhedral dice (41). We have earlier seen how the dominant rules of this consumerist nightworld have required Charlie's only friend, Moe, to beat him, literally, even apparently fatally. The extension of the game beyond a board, to 'our imagination', also reflects how, beyond the world of the characters, McDowall is telling a story, presenting the audience with options for making meanings, from which they can formulate interpretations. Charlie's 'Lovecraftian' RPG seems to take a number of cues from the game 'Call of Cthulhu', first published by Chaosium in 1981, designed by Sandy Petersen and subsequently developed by others; McDowall's play *Pomona* also seems to reflect and extend theatrically Petersen's concept of an 'onion skin' narrative, whereby an initially apparently simple investigation leads to implications in layers of appalling depths, from which the investigator may not be able to return (through a compromise of their sanity, and/or otherwise).

Charlie's gleeful suggestion, that Keaton's use of her own name for that of her player-character will 'make it more immersive' (42), may have unanticipated consequences. Will scene /**nineteen** suggest that Keaton has (in some ways, belatedly) become immersed (surprisingly, even to her) in her game role, prepared to break step/rank and determined to thwart a 'new dark reign'?

Scene /**seven** is the first of two scenes in which McDowall specifies that the dispensation of lines is at the discretion of

the director, creating a process of fluid slippage between
characters (which may theatrically recall the cadences
of Sarah Kane's *Crave*, 1998, or Ed Thomas's *Stone City
Blue*, 2004, also plays of individual disintegration, intense
haunting confrontations and defiant purpose). Ollie acts
out a temporal topography of continuity, succession and
consequence, which becomes increasingly vertiginous and
traumatic. However, the orderly surface cracks, a fissure
appearing in the cheerfully 'strip-lit' and 'colourful' "skin"
of the shopping centre (itself architecturally a consumerist 'loop'), revealing the structural "skull" of a 'shuttered
steel' barn of fundamental interpersonal disconnectivity
(42). The morbid compliance momentarily breaks apart on
a shattering anomaly: Fay is the woman with the laptop,
on the run from Gale and her superiors after the events of
scene /**eleven**. Fay will mistake Ollie for her 'taken' twin,
and see her return as something initially miraculous. However, when Ollie shows no sign of recognizing Fay, Fay
finds the encounter increasingly, maddeningly uncanny and
threateningly 'unimaginable', even as she tries to warn an
uncomprehending Ollie that the forces of Gale's employ-
ers are approaching. Ollie – to whom Fay will appear a
stranger – will also have found the confrontation uncanny
and haunting, but also a telling intimation of the horror and
terror concealed by the city's surface and rhythm. Charlie's 'Lovecraftian' game, set up in rather ludicrously geeky
terms, uncannily yields one of the most deeply Lovecraftian moments in *Pomona*: the sense of a surface of order
cracked by the different act of a different protagonist, which
makes the scene lurch into a lurid multi-dimensional queasy
technicolour.

Scene /**eight** presents a tour de force of scabrous comedy with Charlie unfolding his 'jizz' fantasia with all the playful verve of a 1930s/'40s Walt Disney or Tex Avery cartoon. Charlie's cheerful aria of polymorphous perversity is wildly, hilariously divergent from conventional bids to pass the time through conversation (Moe protests, in attempted but failed containment of the topic's burgeoning, that this is not even 'a conversation', 'just you telling me about your dick'; 50). However, even Charlie's reverie contains a glimpse of latent or implicit dread surrounding physical and mortal limits: the hospital room full of people hidden from general sight, 'with all wires and stuff coming out of them' (49), a foreshadowing of the subterranean labyrinth of horror disclosed in scene /**seventeen**. Gale's brusque terseness introduces a tragicomic pressure to the scene, and her final reference to 'The Girl' introduces a figure whom an alarmed Charlie wants to limit to the boundaries of urban myth: his horror, and the grimness of Gale and Moe, will confirm that he cannot. On many levels, the audience and characters are subject to the opening up of an indeterminate liminal zone where the distinctions between the literal and the fantastic are no longer secure, and from which no exit is possible.

McDowall is highly skilful at establishing a powerful style and mood in the first half of a scene, then realigning the scene, as on a perspectival hinge, so that all involved find themselves in a subversively different, unpredictable terrain. Scene /**eight** took the characters and audience from a precisely timed and weighed double act dealing with matters of ludicrous physicality, into murderous gangster politics, and the first mention of an urban-mythic gothic phantom. Scene /**nine** starts by steadily disclosing gruelling evidence of new depths in human objectification and degradation, which Fay and the audience piece together between the strobe-light flickerings of "Ollie's" words. Then "Ollie's" introduction of the premise that she has a twin sister makes the scene – and its predecessors, particularly /**five** and /**seven** – re-viewable from a radically different perspective, which generates an entirely different chain of possible consequences.

The script version of *Pomona* confirms McDowall's strategic intentions, but only at the end, to be applied and confirmed (as in performance) retrospectively: that in scenes /**five**, /**nine** and /**nineteen**, the actor playing Ollie should also play Ollie's (unnamed) sister. This masterstroke of theatrical *trompe-l'œil* can be viewed in hindsight as a 'prestige' flourish on the part of the dramatist (the culmination of an illusion, as identified and depicted in Christopher Nolan's 2006 sacrificial intrigue film, *The Prestige*). But for the audience – as for the characters – it provokes a jolt of uncertainty, as to who is dreaming who, here. This Ollie-faced twin of scene /**nine** is also a long way from the nervously polite ingénue of scene /**one**, as she savours the details of cutting off the face of an abusive policemen, and reducing everyone and everything in a city to ash. It is additionally enigmatic in posing the question: what further depths might she suspect, that make her so protective as to prohibit anyone to seek her, if she disappears like some of her fellow prostitutes?

Additionally enigmatic further depths are also provided by scene /**ten**, though it is focussed elsewhere, on Charlie and Moe. Their relationship is tragicomic: it embodies the ludicrous comedy of hapless characters trying to respond to the accelerating pace of external directives. The inscrutable forces of competitive performance are tragically destructive and ironic, in that they would conceal their own crimes of human objectification as secrets, whilst themselves resisting the systematic surveillance they enshrine elsewhere. How-ever, tragicomic situations can modulate into full-fledged tragedies, if characters prove able to (re)discover conscious will and agency in their apparently impossible position, and insist on guilt and responsibility in formerly incomprehen-sible and inaccessible hierarchies, by identifying and trans-forming their own former limits, in a defiant resistance of received values (see Rabey, 2015: 9–14 and Botting, 1996: 9). *Pomona* may possibly raise some hopes, at this juncture, that Charlie, Moe and Ollie (and "Ollie") may prove able to do this, if they – and the audience – can penetrate to the root of the increasingly nightmarish landscape and its regulative mysteries. Or else: there is a grimly impending contrary logic emerging, that they will likely become further grist to its mill.

Scene /**eleven** presents another perspective on this unfolding human food chain. Fay and Gale's stand-off has the taut suspense of the *noir* detective thriller, with Gale's keenly cynical observations about Fay's repeated gullibility and neo-masochistic vulnerability attempting to take down Fay's bid to escape with the laptop: a ploy which looks close to succeeding at times, when Fay, initially decisive in her outrage and horror, now hesitates, in reaction to Gale's shrewdly hard-boiled lines and performance.

Scene /**twelve** returns to Charlie and Keaton's RPG ses-sion commenced in scene /**six**, but the enactive avatar of Ollie/Ollie's Twin is no longer present onstage, as she was when that scene modulated mysteriously into scene /**seven**. Partly in consequence of this, the initial tone of scene /**twelve** is a more two-dimensional comedy of role-playing manners, though again the mood will darken unpredictably, as the characters are dilated by their actions and reflections on social contexts. Charlie's initiatives are frequently unsustainable, though their failures are pitiful. Keaton's outburst, insisting that he should not work in Pomona, is significant: though characteristically brusque and unexplained, it indicates concern and an attempted intervention in his (apparent) choices of circumstances. Keaton's reflex back into wanting to play the game is her bid to continue the scene as before, though this proves impossible. Charlie's description of the apparently forgotten and overgrown rewilding 'island' of Pomona adds a mysterious density of texture to the world of the play, and its effect upon Keaton seems significant, but enigmatically so. In retrospect, Charlie's playful evocations of an amoral new age of slavery, indifference to considerations of humanity and the preparation of the 'fruits' of the human body for sacrifice, all foreshadow the shockingly grotesque and macabre developments which Ollie will discover in the depths of this landscape, ironically named after a divine fertility.

Scene /**thirteen** offers a further "thickening" of the world of the play and its narrative weave by bringing together two characters who have not previously been shown together. It also depicts (more remarkably, in an often rapid and violent play) a slow and careful approach to a surprising intimacy, though even this has to emerge from, and overturn, the expectations and values associated by a financial contract which licenses human objectification (McDowall's work often suggests that one of the most important struggles is that against an exclusively dispossessive sense of time). Moe recalls, but ultimately eludes, the identikit features of misogynistic men who have traumatically shaped Fay's reflexes and assumptions: his specific frankness and doubts are what enable him to slip through the net of her condemnation. McDowall's beautifully simple yet infinite stage direction, '*The world falls around them.*' (92), is intended to inspire director and performers to achieve a sense of boundaries collapsing inwards, suggesting the release which might somehow be possible, if and when they can manage to rise above everything that apparently defines their world, in time and space.

Scene /**fourteen** contrastingly shows the difficulty of this, when that world has intricate, surprising and ominous depths. In Ned Bennett's production, a sonic barrage of oppressive technological white noise accompanied the progress across the stage space of the performer of Ollie, who was suddenly briefly illuminated at various junctures (appearing shockingly close to varying audience members in the process); however, she also suddenly appeared at an unexpected position in the space, wearing a hospital gown and a dazed expression – an apparition who could subsequently be interpreted as Ollie's Twin. In my production, our staging in Aberystwyth's Emily Davies Studio permitted the performer of Ollie (Rose Robinson) to emerge from a backlit gallery door situated above and at the back of the main action, and walk around a metal walkway bordering the entire playing area: she shone her torch upward at various industrial-metal tubes and ducts above her, emphasizing both height and depth, before increasing her pace across the full elevated level of the studio space, her boots clattering percussively on the cold metal above the heads of the audience as she disappeared from their view, through a door above and behind them, near to the lighting box. This had the disorientating effect of situating the audience in a depth lower than the action of the protagonist, foreshadowing further disturbing effects of descent and location in scene /**seventeen**.

Scene /**fifteen** is one of *Pomona*'s most disturbing, based on nightmarish reversals which challenge the imagination to keep up with, and complete, violent atrocities which are (wisely) delineated through provocative speech rather than explicit action. This is Gale's sole moment of (awkwardly performed, because uncharacteristic) subjugation (in the ensuing action, staged earlier in scene /**three**, she is fiercely and desperately attempting to wrest back control over her final situation and manner of death). This is the first time we see Keaton speak directly to anyone other than Charlie, though her apparition in scene /**two** implied some of the chilling and lethal power which she now puts into words. Keaton's apparently unsocialized abruptness previously gave her a childlike quality, which Charlie tried to draw out into further interaction. Here, she seems a demonically childish but horrifyingly powerful figure, like an uncannily animated doll who is unstoppably reducing humans to lesser (inanimate) dolls.

It is Moe and Charlie's failure – or rather, refusal – to dispose of Fay in scene /**sixteen** which leads Keaton to pursue Fay personally and confront her in scene /**two**. This bleak irony is paralleled by another, more tragic irony: it is Moe's astonished discovery of profound unease, expressed in scene /**sixteen**, at the thought of Charlie getting killed, that makes him instigate the fiction of Fay's assisted escape: which Moe tries to make convincing by inflicting genuine wounds, which unexpectedly lead to Charlie's death. Moe and Charlie's arresting but initially enigmatic violent harmings in scene /**four** – desperately determined yet not entirely conventionally aggressive – now assume an additional appalling significance, even a failed heroism and strangely tangled homoeroticism: Moe is driving himself to wound Charlie, and be wounded by him, in a bid to keep Charlie alive, the one prospect which gives Moe's life a surprising meaning. However, Moe's anger (which, he has acknowledged, is primarily self-directed) and problems with control may be what proves fatally crucial and self-defeating. This is one of the most brilliant junctures of *Pomona*: how McDowall depicts his characters straining against a world predicated on social and financial determinism, where money is valued over human life, and achieving a brief fragile contrary significance by insisting on separative **consequence**, before they are suddenly swallowed up by the billowing infernal rhythms of their world. The play's whole sequence of dramatic events immediately becomes more significant, and more appalling.

The voice and form of the "dead" Charlie instigates the directive contexts and outcomes for Ollie's exploration of the subterranean labyrinth in scene /**seventeen**, as if to emphasize the chthonic nature of this crucial, in some ways climactic, discovery scene. The ways that all the other characters join him to form a chorus suggests both external pressures and personal disintegration (and so may remind some of the cumulative effects of the distributed lines and words in Sarah Kane's *Crave* and *4.48 Psychosis*); their dogging and challenging the increasingly distraught Ollie also gives them some of the intrigued but detached, superior and merciless, force of classical theatre's furies. The tunnel running below Pomona may initially evoke the underground layer and complex of a James Bond villain or a nightmarish version of Alice's rabbit hole; as it becomes more gothically threatening, the subterranean world becomes closer to that of David Rudkin's *The Sons of Light* (1976), a scientific 'pit' of systematic human disintegration and vivisection; or the "university" which takes its inmates to breaking point in Kane's *Cleansed*; or, ultimately, the looping and churning grey ashen holocaust wasteland of Howard Barker's *Found in the Ground*. McDowall begins the scene by evoking the investigative detail and exciting pace of a fantastic heroic thriller (raising the hope that Ollie will find her sister and somehow defeat the forces of darkness); but he steadily increases the pace, pressure and temperature of flooding nightmare images, which protagonist and audience must try to visualize, manage and navigate, until the enacted and reactive levels of vertiginous desperation become more terrifyingly unmanageable (to the point of this scene becoming capable of inducing empathetic physiological symptoms of dread, even on repeated viewings), before a chillingly abrupt stop.

McDowall's mischievous stage directions for the relative comic relief of scene /**eighteen** sets stimulating challenges for a production team, akin to the open, but definite, prescriptions of the notorious stage directions in Shakespeare's *The Winter's Tale* ('Exit pursued by a bear'), and in Kane's *Phaedra's Love* and *Cleansed*. In Ned Bennett's production of *Pomona*, Guy Rhys as Zeppo signified his transformation by appearing in a white tie and tailcoat from the waist up, replacing his former mac and vest, but retaining his bathetic dirty underpants below that. In our Aberystwyth production, we situated and suddenly illuminated the performers of Charlie and Zeppo apparently in flight, and then squatting, literally and (audibly) startlingly over the heads of audience members, on the trampoline grid of the Emily Davies Studio auditorium. This gave particular poignance and edge to Charlie's sense of separation and Zeppo's superciliousness, respectively, as, suspended in mid-air, they looked down on the audience. Their attitudes are finely poised: Charlie wistfully remembers Keaton as 'this girl', not The Girl; Zeppo, in whatever form, is a nonchalantly insinuating pound-shop Mephistopheles, fundamentally detached and reductive.

Scene /**nineteen** begins with a disorientated figure meeting another, in the rewildings of a cracked landscape. It is a

scene which reminds me of a newly powerful modern version of the blasted heath scene at the heart of Shakespeare's
King Lear (especially if you add a faint whistle of wind to the
soundtrack, as well as the odd distant car, as we did).

It is *possible* to infer that there is only one Ollie: either that
the pull on the leg has awoken an institutionalized patient
("Ollie") from the fantasy of her Mancunian quest (in which
Ollie is an avatar); or that Ollie's Twin is an imaginary projection of a schizophrenic Ollie; or that either or both are
characters in a role-playing game which endlessly reboots,
like a circle of hell, perhaps under the indifferent gaze of
Cthulhu. However, McDowall's (only retrospectively evident) scripted specification as to which character appears in
which scene indicates their separate identities (and accounts
for their different personalities). But, if the quest for a missing sister, and initial encounter with Zeppo, is about to be
"cued" again, is this a deterministic cycle of futility? Or
does it indicate even more nihilistic outcomes, with Ollie's
Twin also threatened by consumption, and other characters
doomed to endless repetition (like the characters in Samuel
Beckett's *Play*)? Or. . .

Is it possible that the introduction of some unforeseeable
(and therefore unforeseen) element will (if not break, then)
alter the loop before it begins? Which characters would
still be present, or unaltered, in a subsequent sequence of
events? Keaton has been (with some justification) regarded
and characterized by others as a judgmental terminator, and
an urban-legendary otherworldly predator (like the protagonist of *Under the Skin*, in Michael Faber's 2000 novel and
Jonathan Glazer's 2013 film). However, her interaction with
Charlie, however stumbling and interrupted, and discovery
of suffering at the loss of her 'friend', seems to have awakened

her to some threshold of destructive moral outrage: which may well in itself prove horrifically apocalyptic.

As a character comments in the tenth episode of the HBO television drama *Westworld* (written by Lisa Joy and Jonathan Nolan, 2016), memories are the first steps to consciousness. A loop of sheer repetition means that characters would not be able to learn from their mistakes, because they cannot remember them. This is the arguably fortunate initial plight of *Westworld*'s robotic "hosts", one of which McDowall's Keaton occasionally resembles. Like the "hosts", she repeatedly observes the sociopathic infantilism which passes for normal, realistic impulses expressed by the ostensibly "human" visitors; until she discerns, and may therefore decide, that choices have meaningful consequences (even or especially if these are painful and fatal ones).

The discovery of memory – and the throw of a dice – can inform improvisation, and bids to avoid predictability, thus breaking the loop of externally prescribed and determined behaviour. Such breaks in the loop are stolen moments, when 'Imperceptible redefinitions occurred/Which at a later date may seem significant' (Barker, 1987: 37). *Pomona* leaves us with new memories: at the very least. . . .

4

Aftershocks and resonances

The evening redness in the North West

Pomona's final scenes raise further questions, as to whether some crucial intervention and salvation has been achieved (and by whom, on whose behalf), or not; and whether the first scene is about to be re/played with similar or possibly differently informed consequences. And it asks the audience: which possibilities would they prefer? And why? To cite a sub-title from Howard Barker's play *Victory* (1983), what might be *their* 'choices in reaction'?

As McDowall comments, '*Pomona* is quite densely plotted, but the play backseats it for the most part: in a lot of scenes, the characters are concerned with other, less immediate things: the plot loads itself into your head, almost without you realising' (McDowall, 2016). As McDowall reflects, on a basic level he was 'writing a play about a woman searching for her sister and the various people she meets along the way'; but that play demonstrates the dramatist's shrewd awareness that the investigative process of 'revealing the past is not dramatic in itself'; and 'By giving you only the bare bones of information, the play allows you to connect the dots in your own way' (McDowall, 2016).

So, how to find form for this energy? McDowall wrote *Pomona* imagining it being performed in the round, as an enclosed and pressurized event that would feel 'like a bullring' (McDowall, 2016). The photographs of Ned Bennett's 2014 Orange Tree staging reflect this pressure: the performers are discomfortingly close to the audience, but sunk slightly beneath the seating level in a tight pit of grimy sand, edged by drainage creating a slight lip on which characters like Zeppo and Cthulhu can perch, to watch Ollie, Fay and Keaton in the small arena. When Bennett's production reached Manchester Royal Exchange, where I saw it in October 2015, the staging had changed: characters initially positioned themselves at the apertures of a seating configuration (made up of canvas chairs), radiating out from a slightly raised central heptagonal drain. When Moe and Charlie fought in scene /**three**, Zeppo (unseen by the characters, but not by the audience) pelted them with lashings of blood, which were scrubbed down into the drain at the end of this scene (implying that this drain might be a sinkhole to further cavernous depths). As the pace of events increased, the characters and scenes seemed to be chasing each other around the central drain like balls on a giant roulette wheel (or car drivers on a ring road).

However, when I first read the script of *Pomona* before seeing it in production, I promptly envisaged something different. Although, four times out of five, my directorial instinct is to rehearse and ultimately present a production in the round, on this occasion the *film noir* atmosphere of the text made me think of characters starkly side-lit, moving in and out of strong lights and deep shadows (consciously influenced by the distinctively powerful *chiaroscuro* lighting designs of Ace McCarron, who was fortuitously able to meet and encourage our lighting designer, Paige Brookes). In our Aberystwyth production, the characters emerged from, and dissolved back into, a receding abyss into which the audience gazed; they were also picked out by light, in denaturalized and antagonistic ways, separating them visually in their contrasting narrative perspectives. Lara Kipp delineates the theatrical effects which may accrue where the unseen and partially visible become at least as significant as what is illuminated:

> the visual contrast of stark side lighting . . . requires active imaginative engagement from the audience whose visual sense has to incorporate both the stage as is visible, and the multiple and diverse scenes the characters [evoke] for each other and the audience over the course of the play. Additionally, lighting serves to carve out in more detail the contrasting materialities of the stage set, the costumes. . . [and] contributes both to the abstraction of the actors' bodies through harsh shadows and the resulting fragmentation of the human form and perhaps more importantly also [the] face, but simultaneously highlights [their] vulnerabilities as they prey, play and construct their separate subject identities in repeated attempts to assert power over one another.
>
> (Kipp, 2017: 116)

We additionally deployed three levels of performance space (ground floor for main action, gantry walkway for Ollie's exploration of the subterranean realm where her twin also appeared in a hospital gown, trampoline grid above the audience for Zeppo and Charlie's seagull scene), suggesting both labyrinthine depths and the unlocking of different 'levels' as in the progression of a role-playing game (thanks to Rachel

Smith for this observation). Moreover, each character except Ollie/Ollie's Twin was doubled by two performers, rendering Ollie and "Ollie" more anomalously single and severed, and permitting opportunities for physicalizing the conflicting impulses of other characters, informing each speech and action. This manifested physically Artaud's proposition that everything 'has a shadow which is its double', and that the distinctive power of the medium of theatre, ideally deployed, is its capacity for 'naming and directing shadows' (Artaud, 1938: 12). The soundscape for our production incorporated samples from Barry Adamson's simultaneously exhilarating and deliberately seedy "soundtrack for an imaginary film" set in Manchester, *Moss Side Story*.

One of McDowall's distinctive characteristics as a dramatist is his incorporation of fantastic and (sometimes nightmarishly) transformative effects, which offer something hauntingly unsettling, rather than the escapist wish-fulfilment with which these effects might conventionally be associated. McDowall's plays, *Captain Amazing, Brilliant Adventures* and *X*, provide further examples of this. His theatre should rather be considered a part of an unconventionally deeper, darker romantic impulse and tradition in imaginative writing and performance. Marina Warner reports how W. H. Auden adopted the term 'Secondary World' from Tolkien and C. S. Lewis, to distinguish between 'the Primary, everyday, world' as what is habitually, superficially recognized and known by the individual through the senses; and 'a Secondary world or worlds' which the individual 'not only can create' through personal imagination, but also 'cannot stop' her/himself creating (Warner, 2014: 4) in the process of seeking knowledge. Warner identifies such secondary worlds, whether benign or sinister, as 'laboratories for experiments with thought', speculations into possibilities by way of 'fantastic horizons' which are 'fraught with the unknown or the intimated', 'by definition operating along mysterious lines, organized according to principles that differ from ordinary life', yet which *refract* ordinary life, in zones 'populated by imaginary alter egos, dream selves, and saviour figures, often in the shape of a child quester, who faces ordeals and enemies within and without' (Warner, 2014: 5). These zones are the realm of the uncanny, where 'the banal' discloses 'terrible secrets' (Warner, 2014: 112), but these are nevertheless necessary components of deep knowledge. Warner makes a further important distinction: unlike 'myths, which are about gods and superheroes, fairytale protagonists are recognizably ordinary working people'; in 'fairy tales, want stalks everyone, and the word's double meaning matters: both desire and lack' (Warner, 2014: 78). This is pertinent to the embattled craving which unites all characters in *Pomona*, struggling to make a living on the streets of Manchester, in a recognizably mean time, with Ollie providing the more innocent or naïve figure of the child quester, attempting to navigate this fluctuating terrain and rescue her twin, but – like Lewis Carroll's Alice – beset by grotesques and riddles in her encounters. However, the recurrent invocation and/or presence of the figure of Cthulhu edges the play towards the mythic, perhaps even the metaphysical: without forgetting that *Pomona* takes at least one cue from the popularity of the RPG 'Call of Cthulhu', one may also recall that much of 'Greek theatre, and of Greek mythology in general, hinges upon the drama that happens whenever the gods, the ultimate outsiders, roam among mortals' (Young, 2013: 22). *Pomona* implies that it is the systematization of human indifference which has accordingly let in its appropriate presiding deity.

Antonin Artaud claimed that theatre was the primal form through which to manifest an appropriately new sense of mythic terror, through linguistic and spatial imagery. Indeed, Artaud proposed that 'theatre can only happen the moment the inconceivable really begins', by manifesting 'incredible images giving existence and credibility' to acts which did not literally re-present the surface appearances of social life, but which intended deeper, excavatory import. Therefore, Artaud likened theatre to the catastrophic, convulsive, contagious power of an outbreak of plague, providing an upheaval of conventional social priorities and offering 'a revelation' which involves 'the exteriorisation of a latent undercurrent of cruelty through which all the perversity of which the mind is capable, whether in a person or a nation, becomes localized' (Artaud, 1989: 116). This is in order to lead us 'to reject man's usual limitations and powers', and extend infinitely 'the frontiers of what we call reality' (129); indeed, Artaud insists that it is by introducing on stage 'the irrational and monstrous logic of dreams' (139), that theatre may 'become a kind of experimental manifestation of the deep-seated identity between the abstract and the concrete' (113) and so trigger what McDowall invokes, the unforgettable and irreducible theatrical experience which can only be described in terms of 'being in *that room* with *that thing*'. These objectives have dimensions and resonances which are indeed political, sexual, metaphysical, psychological and philosophical: in total, they are existential.

Pomona sets up a startling montage, plunging into a series of enigmatic high-stake scenes which arouse and compel curiosity by depicting the emotional and psychological states of the characters *in extremis*. It does so in ways which might be identified as distinctly Gothic (and perhaps, in Barker's term, catastrophist), by involving the contestation and dissolution of boundaries, making apparent the possibilities that *anything* can happen, unpredictably. M. J. A. Green suggests that 'we can define the Gothic text as manifesting an uncanny temporal disjunction that disrupts mundane experience to expose the innermost vulnerabilities of the self (the abject)' (Green, 2013: 16, 17), in order to probe matters of social concern, in ways which open up questions about the possible source and nature of evil. It is strangely significant that Alan Moore – a writer who seems to me one of the closest to McDowall in his initiatives and accomplishments – has also chosen to invoke and project the motifs and mythology of Lovecraft in his recent works with Jacen Burrows, *Neonomicon* (2011) and *Providence* (2017). Specifically, the second volume of *Providence* (Moore and Burrows, 2017b) serves to remind us of H. P. Lovecraft's fictional annexation of the American city of Manchester, New Hampshire, to furnish aspects of environs of his fictional Arkham. In *Pomona*, McDowall conjectures what might happen if Lovecraft's Cthulhu appeared in the landscape of Manchester, England, rather than Manchester, New England.

Gale's enraged reflection that she 'hired the *fucking* Marx Brothers' (25) is a withering dismissal of the trustworthiness and competence of Moe and Charlie. However, it is Zeppo whose name directly references a member of that comic team, and it is McDowall's puckish joke that all of the characters of *Pomona* have names associated with famous film clowns: Ollie (Hardy), (Buster) Keaton, Charlie (Chaplin), Moe (Howard/Horwitz, who played the marginally less stupid member of The Three Stooges), Fay (Tincher), Gale (Henry). This parallels Mark Ravenhill's wry decision to name the characters in his breakthrough Royal Court play,

Shopping and Fucking (1996), after members of the band Take That, plus their one-off collaborator Lulu. Indeed, *Pomona* appears to present a further homage/riposte to *Shopping and Fucking* by beginning with a similar premise: a stylishly heartless businessman recounts admiringly but idiosyncratically his interpretation of the plot of a popular movie (in Ravenhill's play, *The Lion King*: thanks to Michael Mangan for this observation). I have noted elsewhere how *Shopping and Fucking* stages 'loosely but rhetorically connected, nihilistically comic juxtapositions', 'studied observations of resolute superficiality' which 'show up the reductivity of 1990s consumerism as both blackly humorous and ultimately lethal' (Rabey, 2003: 202). Thus, *Pomona*'s opening scene contains what may be McDowall's joke, or challenge, or both, to himself: to deploy a similar opening narrative device as a springboard into a 21st century excoriation of human objectification, to be pursued in more surreal, frenetic and fantastic terms than Ravenhill's play of shockingly "cool" systematic detachment. Indeed, McDowall's *Pomona* uses gothic developments of hard-boiled detective and thriller narrative devices, and surprising disclosures of depths in character and landscape, to construct a play which is defiantly, pulsingly "hot".

There are further contact points between *Pomona* and other groundbreaking contemporary plays. In scene /**five**, Ollie's identification of 'a camera', probably situated in the audience area, may recall the strip club scene in Patrick Marber's *Closer* (1997) which also stages the voyeurism and mockery involved in commercializing the promise of intimacy. Moe and Charlie may recall the protagonists of Harold Pinter's *The Dumb Waiter* (1960): double-act hitmen whose occasionally childlike relationship is subjected to lethal instrumentalization, when they are set against and upon each other by their

superiors; they may also remind some of the two assassins in
Martin McDonagh's darkly comic film *In Bruges* (2008), in
which two increasingly reluctant killers become more engaging, as their actions and circumstances become more surreal
and outlandish, because of how their conditions of power
impose a tragicomic restriction of choice under pressure.
Charlie's confession of how he was unjustly associated with a
friend who perpetrated a school shooting may bring to mind
Simon Stephens's *Punk Rock* (first staged at Manchester Royal
Exchange, 2009). Moe's question, 'Do you know what a
snuff film is?' (72), may evoke the unforgettable details of
Sarah Daniels's play *Masterpieces* (Royal Court, 1983), and his
later moment of angry despair, 'It's just a cycle of shit' (102),
echoes a powerful verbal motif in debbie tucker green's *random* (Royal Court, 2008). Charlie's childlike excitement at
the sight of Gale's car may recall Baby's similar thrill at seeing
a Buick in Jez Butterworth's *Mojo* (1995). The underground
vivisection complex of scene /**seventeen** may remind some
of the 'university' compound in Sarah Kane's *Cleansed* (Royal
Court, 1998), though for me it recalls primarily the subterranean disclosures and Promethean odyssey of one of the
most profoundly troubling and stirring plays that I have read
and directed: David Rudkin's *The Sons of Light* (1976, Royal
Shakespeare Company 1977).

   This is not to suggest that *Pomona* is a derivative work.
Indeed, my comparison to Rudkin and *The Sons of Light* is
intended as one of the highest compliments I can bestow,
in terms of truly groundbreaking and unforgettable theatre (McDowall read *The Sons* for the first time in 2017).
McDowall could never be convincingly called 'naïve' as
a dramatist, but my intention here is to contextualize his
work amongst startling effects in other exceptional plays,

and to note how he has made something that is itself exceptional and original in its pursuits. I was tempted to identify McDowall's extrapolation from Stephens's *Punk Rock* as the mark of a younger writer, furthering the inventions of his mentor, in active demonstrations of both homage and daring, and the riff on *Shopping and Fucking* and the echo of *random* as akin to a jazz musician's respectful and witty "quotation" of another's compositional work in an inventive solo. However, McDowall states that these plays were not conscious reference points for him when writing, though he is frank and disarming about the importance of inspirational influences on his work, which should include two notable 'nightmare odyssey' plays: Büchner's *Woyzeck* and David Mamet's *Edmond*. However, important influences were not only theatrical ones: the shootings at Columbine High School in Colorado and Virginia Tech are traumatic events of fearsome resonance. McDowall observes:

> I think the only reason people have thought any of my work was even remotely original is that because my range of influences is perhaps a bit broader. In *Pomona* I'm trying to tap into a certain sense of anxiety and foreboding and dread that sits just under the surface of life; and I find Lovecraft was trying to do the same thing with his Cthulhu mythos. If I put *that* under the play, it'll maybe help people tune in to it. I'm not searching for "a weird thing" to make the play more interesting, I'm looking for the most direct language. In writing *Pomona* I find there's this character in the back with the Cthulhu mask on, initially I don't know why, but I'm going to find out as I work on it by tracing that line back to my subconscious. If I'm writing well, it feels like discovery rather

than invention. Keaton is this kind of angel of death who marauds over everything, so there's a hint of *Akira* in there, and other Japanese anime and manga – how kids in those stories often have this godlike potential: the world in their hands. I also love Cormac McCarthy and how his characters are kind of carved out of the landscape. The Judge in *Blood Meridian* seems like he's *walked out of the stone*. I thought, that's interesting: what if this character Keaton has emerged out of the landscape too, the physical rock and dust and canals of Manchester, but also the cultural landscape. At the same time, she is developed in all the usual ways a character should be. Probably the most interesting thing about her is how she becomes, I hope, one of the most empathetic characters in the play, so you end up caring for her despite the fact that she leads people to appalling deaths.

(McDowall, 2016)

McDowall also notes how other American novelists, such as William Faulkner and Thomas Pynchon, have also been inspirational to him:

Pynchon wrote a lot of big novels in which there is a search for "a thing", but is the thing important? We don't know. What is the thing? We don't really know. What does the thing mean? We don't know. Maybe we'll never know. And maybe half the time we won't even be searching for the thing. He creates tangents within tangents within tangents which both creates and disrupts meaning. I feel like he's come the closest to writing about what 'now' feels like, despite writing the novels where he does this the most in the 1960s and 70s: *The Crying of Lot 49,*

V, Gravity's Rainbow feel like the internet to me, full of chaotic narratives of intricacy and mess, piling up information, everything happening at the same time, with no chance of decoding it at all. I love that. And I think that *Pomona* is partly about the internet, even though no one really mentions it much: about how we live now and how that's been altered by the internet. It's also a play about consumption, people becoming units rather than people, about how everything is bought and sold, bought and sold, in different windows, all playing at the same time.

(McDowall, 2016)

It may be appropriate to return to a starting point, and differentiate. The neo-*noir* world of Roman Polanski's 1974 film *Chinatown* depicts the (disingenuously sunny) outskirts of Los Angeles as a bridge-dominated landscape which is an odd mix of sterility and fertility, spattered with the surreal details of rough sleeping encampments, a gated wire perimeter where people only *think* they know what they are dealing with, and a sense of conventional and genre morality is ultimately flouted, although some characters – and the audience – are made witness to the true horrifying depths of corruption. These motifs and effects are given a specifically English (less sunlit) setting, dimensions and resonances by McDowall in *Pomona*. The figure of McDowall's heroine is also fractured into an enigmatic boundary-blurring conservative/transgressive figure (or figures), in ways which seem to extrapolate the challenging dualities of gothic fiction and *film noir*. Importantly, McDowall creates a strikingly original *theatrical* form, appropriate to his themes: as my 'looping' commentary has aimed to demonstrate.

Markus Oppolzer's essay, on 'Gothic Liminality' in Alan Moore and David Lloyd's graphic novel series *V for Vendetta*, also identifies some concepts which seem pertinent to *Pomona*. Oppolzer notes how most protagonists of Gothic fiction 'have to face the threat of becoming permanently lost in the liminal sphere' of 'separation, transition and incorporation'; and while liminality traditionally 'represents a transitional and voluntary stage in successful rites of passage, it threatens to become a permanent and involuntary state in Gothic narratives' (Oppolzer, 2013: 104). Such narratives manifest how the surface rule of law is nevertheless haunted by characters and phenomena that 'do not − or are not permitted to − fit in, that exist in the liminal areas of society, in its crevices and folds', characters who may (like McDowall's Fay and Charlie) be eager to 'regain some foothold in the social order' and a sense of private autonomy, but who find that 'the extraordinary circumstances of their lives − and especially their liminal and thus unofficial status − prevent such a proceeding' (105). This voracious liminality may ultimately consign such characters to segregation into the 'civil death' of enclosure in a 'total institution' characterized by 'locked doors, high walls, barbed wire, cliffs, water, forests, or moors' necessary to effect the 'transition from person to patient' and part of the 'research stock' (Oppolzer, 2013: 106, drawing on terms from Erving Goffman).

However, Oppolzer notes that Moore's protagonist, V, achieves a dramatic rebirth and escape through motifs of fire and destruction, and so 'becomes a complete anomaly: he exists physically and legally outside the system, a ghostlike presence on the fringe of society into whose classificatory system he no longer fits' (107–8). Such a revenant apparition raises fundamental questions:

> to what degree are we willing to compromise to fit into the pre-existing subject positions offered by various

institutions? How does a society deal with its liminal sphere, the unstructured space outside its classificatory system, where some individuals are forced to exist? Where do the personal liberties of individuals end?

(Oppolzer, 2013: 115)

I refer finally to Polanski's *Chinatown* and Moore and Lloyd's *V for Vendetta* to draw parallels with, but also to note the significant differences of, McDowall's *Pomona*. If Ollie's self-sacrifice does manage to liberate her bewildered twin, then possibility of redemption is horrifying and tragic, but not impossible (so that not all of McDowall's characters are, like the investigator of *Chinatown*, 'forever stuck in liminality', powerless and 'condemned only to repeat'; Eaton, 1997: 71). However, if Ollie is indeed doomed to a nightmarishly Promethean consumption in the underworld, *Pomona* appallingly subverts the triumph of the detective and superhero. It may be that possibilities are triggered by Ollie's staggeringly persistent unselfishness, so that her twin, and perhaps even Keaton, may be able to instigate further violent rebirths, perhaps involving the scenarios of fiery destruction that they have both entertained. Whether or not their actions involve further destruction, Ollie's twin and Keaton might, at least, discover and embody some newly significant form of agency, in and through their realm of anomaly.

Moreover, *Pomona* asks: if these characters are "living in a simulation" (and they manifestly are, on at least one level, by being on a stage!), then what are *we* doing? Are we telling our own stories, or populating the prewritten and atomizing scenarios of those who purport and intend to run the world? How should we begin to tell engaging and surprising new stories, of what it is to be a human in 21st-century Britain?

Pomona – like McDowall's other plays – suggests that the acknowledgment of suffering is a necessary key to awakening, and breaking the self-defeating loop of determinism. McDowall's theatre is both horizontal and vertical in its imaginative reach: it takes vivid account of restricted space, and plunges downward into hellish depths, discovering political metaphors for the present-day social experiences. However, the sacrificial narrative of *Pomona* does not operate at a formal metaphorical remove from the present tense: part of its horror springs from its manifest incorporation (and projection) of immediate tensions and details which can be identified in dysfunctional forms of urban community. *Pomona* is a howl (no less than Allen Ginsberg's poem) against human objectification and *waste*: the sacrifice and loss of human potential (most starkly embodied by the tragic fates of Ollie and Charlie), and the reduction, in the nightmare underground world, of human bodies to commodities, units to be traded or "fracked" to exhaustion, where the only value of a principle or an action seems systematically reduced to its economic outcome. Within this visceral twilight world, *Pomona* nevertheless also gives brief but defiantly memorable status and powers of expression to lost souls, including addicted prostitutes and aimless security guards, in ways which will make audiences remember them as human beings with rights and hopes, as well as what they are expected and made to endure, in the marginalized territories to which they are consigned.

Moreover, *Pomona* insists that our human choices will have, must have, consequences; that you can write your own story; and that you can wise up, and take the game apart.

References

Artaud, Antonin (1938) *The Theatre and Its Double*, trans. M. C. Richards. New York: Grove.

Artaud, Antonin (1989) *Artaud on Theatre*, ed. Claude Schumacher. London: Methuen.

Baldick, Chris (1992) 'Introduction', in C. Baldick (ed.), *The Oxford Book of Gothic Tales*. Oxford: Oxford University Press, pp. xi–xxiii.

Barker, Howard (1987) *Gary the Thief/Gary Upright*. London: John Calder.

Barker, Howard (2016) *Arguments for a Theatre* (4th edition). London: Oberon.

Botting, Fred (1996) *Gothic*. Abingdon: Routledge.

Clements, Rachel (2015) 'Waking Nightmares Inside the M60', Programme Essay for Manchester Royal Exchange production, 29 October–21 November 2015.

Eaton, Michael (1997) *Chinatown*. London: BFI.

Edgar, David (2009) *How Plays Work*. London: NHB.

Farley, Paul and Roberts, Michael Symmons (2012) *Edgelands*. London: Vintage.

Green, Matthew J. A. (ed.) (2013) *Alan Moore and the Gothic Tradition*. Manchester: Manchester University Press.

Horner, Avril and Zlosnik, Sue (2005) *Gothic and the Comic Turn*. Basingstoke: Palgrave Macmillan.

Jenks, Chris (1995) 'Watching Your Step', in Chris Jenks (ed.), *Visual Culture*. London and New York: Routledge, pp. 142–150.

Kipp, Lara Maleen (2017) *The Scenographic Sublime: An Aesthetic Analysis of Howard Barker's Work 1998–2011*. PhD thesis: Aberystwyth University.

Kirby, Dean (2016) 'Homeless People in Manchester Sleeping in Victorian-Style Secret Subterranean "Cave"', *The Independent* 29/01/2016 www.independent.co.uk/news/uk/home-news/homeless-people-in-manchester-sleeping-in-victorian-style-secret-subterranean-cave-a6842501.html accessed 06/07/2017.

Lovecraft, H. P. (1999) *The Call of Cthulhu and Other Weird Stories* ed. S. T. Joshi. London: Penguin.

Mamet, David (2010) *Theatre*. London: Methuen.

McDowall, Alistair (2016) In Conversation with David Ian Rabey, Dialogues in Contemporary Theatre no. 1, Aberystwyth University Department of Theatre, Film and Television Studies, 2/11/2016. Suggested addition: Transcript of an audio recording of interview, extracts slightly amended for publication.

McFarlane, Robert (2015) 'The Eeriness of the English Countryside', *The Guardian* 10/04/2015 www.theguardian.com/books/2015/apr/10/eeriness-english-countryside-robert-macfarlane accessed 01/11/2016.

Mitchell, David (2015) *Slade House*. London: Sceptre.

Moore, Alan and Burrows, Jacen (2011) *Neonomicon*. Rantoul: Avatar.

Moore, Alan and Burrows, Jacen (2017a) *Providence Act 1*. Rantoul: Avatar.

Moore, Alan and Burrows, Jacen (2017b) *Providence Act 2*. Rantoul: Avatar.

Oppolzer, Marcus (2013) 'Gothic Liminality in *V for Vendetta*', in Green, Michael J. A. (ed.), *Alan Moore and the Gothic Tradition*. Manchester: Manchester University Press, pp. 103–117.

Rabey, David Ian (2003) *English Drama Since 1940*. Harlow: Longman/Pearson.

Rabey, David Ian (2015) *The Theatre and Films of Jez Butterworth*. London: Bloomsbury.

Rebellato, Dan (2014) *Pomona*, www.danrebellato.co.uk/spilledink/2014/11/22/pomona accessed 06/07/2017.

Robinson, Ken (2011) *Out of Our Minds: Learning to be Creative* (2nd edition). Chichester: Capstone.

Trueman, Matt (2014) 'Alistair McDowall: "There Are No Rules in Theatre – You Can Do Anything"', *The Guardian* 26/04/2014 www.theguardian.com/stage/2014/apr/26/alistair-mcdowall-rules-theatre-anything accessed 06/07/2017.

Turner, Victor (1997) *The Ritual Process: Structure and Anti-Structure*. New York: Aldine de Gruyter.

Warner, Marina (2014) *Once Upon a Time*. Oxford: Oxford UP.

Williams, Holly (2016) 'Alistair McDowall' interview, *The Independent* 20/03/2016 www.independent.co.uk/arts-entertainment/theatre-dance/features/alistair-mcdowall-the-future-of-british-theatre-on-setting-a-play-on-pluto-and-sympathising-with-his-a6939136.html accessed 02/11/2016.

Young, Harvey (2013) *Theatre & Race*. Basingstoke: Palgrave Macmillan.

Index

T - #0162 - 130720 - C0 - 172/119/5 - PB - 9781138235298